Cat Scene Investigator:
Solve Your Cat's Litter Box Mystery

Dusty Rainbolt, ACCBC

Stupid Gravity Press, LLC
Lewisville, Texas

DEDICATION

To Nixie, who patiently taught me so much,
My hero and husband, Weems,
And Cindy Rigoni and Beth Adelman—
God sent you all to help cats.

CONTENTS

Acknowledgments   i
Foreword   iii
Introduction   v

1   An Overview: Procedures for Fighting Slime   Pg   1
2   Gathering Evidence & Looking for Motive   Pg   5
3   Is It Peeing or Marking?   Pg 11
4   Whodunit? Apprehending the Suspect(s) in a Multipet Home   Pg 15
5   Caught in the Act   Pg 19
6   Thinking Inside the Litter Box   Pg 23
7   Crime Scene Cleanup   Pg 43
8   Cat Tagging: When Kitty Marks   Pg 53
9   Hurry Up in There! Potty Issues in the Multipet Home   Pg 69
10 So Sick It's Criminal: Feline Lower Urinary Tract Disease   Pg 81
11 So Sick It's Criminal: Everything Else   Pg 97
12 Senior Moments   Pg 119
13 Environmental Enrichment: Just What the Doctor Ordered   Pg 143
14 Outside Cats and Restraining Orders   Pg 159
15 Litter Box Rehab   Pg 165
16 When All Else Fails   Pg 173
    Reader Resources   Pg 181
    Selected Works Cited   Pg 183
    Index   Pg 195
    About the Author   Pg 203

ACKNOWLEDGMENTS

Photos: Weems S. Hutto; Beth Adelman (pages 30 and 128); Patton at the Rhine (page 54) courtesy of the *Weekly Standard;* Candi Smith (page 140), and Mugsy and the Alligator (page 63) courtesy of Lori C. Blair and Cajun Pride Swamp Tours; Feline Lifestages Chart (page 120) courtesy of Arnold Plotnick, MD, DVM, ACVIM and the Manhattan Cat Hospital

Foreword: Marty Becker, DVM

Technical editors: C.A. Tony Buffington, DVM, PhD, DACVN; Cynthia Rigoni, DVM and Beth Adelman, MS

Copy editor: Ruthanne Brockway

Proofreader: Marci Kladnik

Cartoons: Stephanie Piro

Illustrations: Pat Jackson

Cover photos: Weems S. Hutto

Cover design: Alerrandre

There were so many people who helped make this book a reality. Additional thanks goes to the vets, behaviorists and cat owners who provided invaluable interviews: Beth Adelman, MS; Joan and Chris Browne, Ahna Brutlag, DVM, MS, DABT, DABVT; Nicholas H. Dodman, BVMS, MRCVS; Robin Downing, DVM, DAAPM, DACVSMR, CVPP, CCRP; Michael W. Dryden, DVM, PhD; Cassie Epstein, DVM; Lorie Huston, DVM; Susan Konecny, RN, DVM; Marci L. Koski, PhD; Diane Levitan, VMD, Dip ACVIM; Susan Little, DVM, DABVP; Jennifer Mauger CPDT-KSA, Mieshelle Nagelschneider, Judy Morgan DVM, CVA, CVCP, CVFT; Jacqueline Munera, CCBC, PCBC, CAP; Tom Nelson, DVM; Kim Nestor, Niwako Ogata, BVSc, PhD, DACVB; Lauren-Ashley Oliver; Pet Poison Helpline; Art Rainbolt; The Rainbolt Test Kitties, CATS; Roberta Relford, DVM, MS, PhD, DACVIM, DAVCP; Cynthia Rigoni, DVM; Linda Ross, DVM, MS, DACVIM; Margie Scherk, DVM, ABV; Carlo Siracusa, DVM, PhD, MS; Candi Smith, Chris Smits, Drew Weigner, DVM, ABVP; Sophia Yin, DVM, MS; and Anne M. Zajac, DVM, PhD, DACVM.

Also thank you for technical and emotional support: Deb Barnes, Carole Nelson Douglas (Wishlist Publishing), Caroline Golon, Kim Innes, Jennifer from Arizona, Janiss Garza, Marci Kladnik, Larry and Julia Mandala (Fantasy Writers Asylum), Arden Moore, Pat Chapman, Margaret Rainbolt,

CAT SCENE INVESTIGATOR

Selina and Lynn Rosen (Yard Dog Press), Chris Ruben, Amy D Shojai, CABC, Kim Campbell Thornton, Debbie Waller, James Woodruff and Gina Zaro.

FOREWORD

We invite cats into our homes because we want to experience that special bond only pets can provide—a bond of trust, affection and mutual respect. When cats begin eliminating outside the litter box that bond is broken. In the eyes of both human and cat, trust breaks down. Fear takes its place.

A few years ago I launched the Fear Free Initiative, a program that transforms vet visits from a terrifying journey, where the cat is manhandled, prodded and violated, into a calm experience, where treats and massages camouflage what were once invasive procedures.

Fear Free starts at home. Every cat should be able to use the litter box without fear of pain, attack or revulsion. Very often, housesoiling begins with an illness or fear.

Cat Scene Investigator: Solve Your Cat's Litter Box Mystery is a must-read book for every cat owner. Using her trademark humorous approach, Dusty Rainbolt will help you view things with a detective's eye to determine and correct the cause of housesoiling, or better still, to prevent the problem entirely.

With trust restored, fear vanishes. It's a happy ending for everyone, including your carpet.

Dr. Marty Becker
America's Veterinarian

CAT SCENE INVESTIGATOR

"You might want to put this on before you come inside. I'm having a little trouble with my cat!"

INTRODUCTION

A cat is the only domestic animal I know who toilet trains itself and does a damned impressive job of it. ~Joseph Epstein

Who hasn't visited a cat lover's home and inhaled a lungful of ammonia? Ah, Eau de Toilette Félin. Your friend holds out a World War II gas mask, saying, "You might want to put this on before you come inside. I'm having a little trouble with my cat."

Since you're reading this book, I'm betting you wish you had a gas mask of your own.

Are you considering surrendering your cat to an animal shelter or putting him to sleep? Wait! Getting rid of the cat isn't the answer. The problem will persist long after the perpetrator has left your home. Imperceptible pee clings to surfaces, posting an invisible olfactory sign that instructs any new pet (both cat and dog) to, "Pee here."

There is hope. You *can* reform your cat and rid your home of the odor of cat pee. Even the most odoriferous home can be restored to a pollution-free zone.

Before you reply, "That's easy for you to say," please understand, I've been in your pee-covered shoes. If I escaped the smell of ammonia, you can too.

To uncover the causes and answers for housesoiling I studied feline behavior, attended veterinary conferences and joined the International Association of Animal Behavior Consultants. I interviewed the planet's top veterinarians and behaviorists and scoured countless research papers and veterinary proceedings. I'm sharing what I discovered with you.

As the former product editor of *Catnip* (the Tufts University of Veterinary Medicine newsletter), The Rainbolt Test Kitties, my hard-working team of product testers, helped me conduct unscientific preference, safety and utility evaluations of everything feline. We still review products and post the results on my website: DustyCatWriter.com. Because I test so many fabulous (and not so successful) products, I'm sharing the ones the Test Kitties and I thought would be most helpful to you. In the spirit of full disclosure, I must tell you that many of the products included in this book and on my website were sent as samples. But I never write about anything that doesn't pass feline muster with flying colors.

I'll walk you through the process of regaining your home and help you rekindle your love affair with your kitty. Take a deep breath. I smell fresh air in your future

1   AN OVERVIEW: PROCEDURES FOR FIGHTING SLIME

*As anyone who has ever been around a cat for any length of time well knows,
cats have enormous patience with the limitations of the human mind.*
~ Cleveland Amory

There's a turf war going on inside your home. It's time to draw a line in the sandbox and end the hostilities.

Inappropriate elimination is more complicated than a congressional health-care bill. To arrive at a fresh smelling home, you'll need to:

• Figure out who's making the mess (if you have a multipet home)

1

- Take your kitty to the vet
- Determine if he's marking or going to the bathroom
- Find out what's upsetting your cat
- Fix it
- Retrain him
- Find all the soiled spots
- Remove the smell of pee from the floors and walls
- Make the target area unattractive
- Enjoy the new feeling of calm

Remember, your cat isn't the Public Enemy Number One. He can more accurately be described as a hostage. He wants a resolution as much as you do. So I'm going to show you how to get your house and your beloved cat back.

Use this book as a cop would use any procedural manual.

For simplicity's sake, in *Cat Scene Investigator* (*CSI*), Fluffy is my Every Cat. I refer to him as male. In situations that only apply to females or only to males, I'll alert you.

CSI contains a number of icons to help you navigate this book, including:

[WARNING!] Don't ignore this icon. This alerts you that something could be extremely hazardous or deadly to your cat or yourself.

⚠ cautions that something could cause damage inside your home.

❧ This is the Rainbolt Test Kitties' Pawprint of Approval. These are products that my cats and I found to work. Of course every cat and every home is different, so nothing works for everyone in every situation.

Stopping a crime spree takes strategy, planning and a coordinated effort. Ground will be lost and gained. Some things will work, some won't. You may suffer temporary defeats. If that happens, you fall back, regroup, and come up with Plan B or Plan D or Plan Z. You'll have to fight this campaign on several fronts at the same time. With persistence and patience you'll win the day.

We're still early in the book, but I'm going to repeat this point throughout: It's crucial to take your cat to the vet as soon as you notice a mistake. You can't skip this step. Peeing or pooping outside the litter box can be a sign of numerous medical conditions. And if it's a medical problem, only your veterinarian can fix it.

After your visit to the vet, it's time to eradicate the odor, not just the stain. You may think by squirting some enzyme or bacteria-based cleaner on the stain, voilà, it's clean. Unfortunately, some cleaning products take up to 72 hours to break down odor molecules. That's written in fine print on the label. If the carpet dries before they've finished their job, they quit working. The pee continues to linger in the carpet padding and subflooring like an embarrassing photo on the internet. To your kitty's sensitive nose, that quiet corner still smells like a latrine. And baby, if it smells like a bathroom, it's still open for business!

Don't panic, and don't give up. I'll guide you to your destination in the state of Calm and Fresh. Kiss your cat. Put on your rubber gloves. It's time to get started. You are now officially a Cat Scene Investigator.

2   GATHERING EVIDENCE & LOOKING FOR MOTIVE

No cat can be expected to use a litter box if it gives her an anxiety attack. We all need a little peace and quiet when we are in that most vulnerable position. ~ Beth Adelman

It doesn't matter whether your favorite detective is Thomas Magnum, Sherlock Holmes, James Qwilleran, Leroy Jethro Gibbs, or Midnight Louie, they all use the power of observation to crack a case. They also ask a lot of questions. Crime scene investigators view security video, take photos, draw diagrams, analyze blood splatter patterns, and determine trajectory angles. They look at the placement of the furniture and check the doors and windows for signs of intruders. Cat scene investigators do the same thing. Many inappropriate elimination problems are easily solved after collecting clues about your suspect and his surroundings.

If you really want to know why your cat has an elimination problem, take a few minutes to answer this questionnaire and diagram your home before you read the rest of this book. Your answers will provide helpful information to you, your vet and a behaviorist (if you need one later). Think about the questions listed below as they relate to all of your cats. If you don't know the answers now, come back to them later. If you can't print it off, go to http://dustycatwriter.com/nv_dusty/cat-scene-investigator-solve-your-cats-litter-box-mystery/csi-questionaire/ and download the list. Password: GoodFluffy.

Keep the list near you as you read *Cat Scene Investigator*. Your honest answers will help address specific problems.

I urge you, let go of your preconception about your cat's motives for missing the box. Read this book with an open mind.

Recently, a lady asked, "Why is my cat suddenly too good to squat in the box?" She was upset because her 8-year-old cat, who had once squatted to go to the bathroom, now stands and shoots pee over the litter pan onto the wall and floor. When I suggested she take the cat to the vet because he may be suffering from arthritis, she insisted he couldn't possibly have achy joints because he still jumped on the counter. Cats are naturally secretive about pain or illness, so I explained jumping takes only a fraction of a second, whereas squatting to pee or poop requires a kitty maintaining a painful position for 30 to 60 seconds. I suggested *she* try crouching for one minute. Only then did she realize her kitty may no longer be able to assume a squat.

This woman isn't alone. Often people who ask for my help maintain that the cat misses the box or sprays out of spite, when the likely cause is pain or fear.

Even though we humans were smart enough to land on the moon and invent the can opener, when it comes to bi-species communications, we're sadly lacking. We often misinterpret what our kitties are trying to tell us. It's like actor Strother Martin said to Paul Newman in the movie, *Cool Hand Luke*: "What we have here is a failure to communicate."

Rather than viewing a cat's motive for any infraction as an act of jealousy, anger, stubbornness or arrogance, try looking at it as an attempt to communicate with you. He can't tell you his bladder hurts or he's afraid or the smell of the box makes him queasy.

Hopefully, as you read *CSI* with an open mind and your questionnaire handy, you'll experience some "aha" moments.

Crime Scene Diagram

Let's start with a cat scene diagram of every room your cat has access to. Don't worry about drawing it to scale. Items you need to include are the locations of:

• Litter boxes

- Windows and doors
- Food and water bowls
- All major appliances (washer, dryer, refrigerator, trash compactor, air conditioner, furnace, etc.)
    - Heater and air conditioner vents
    - Locations where Fluffy is spraying/peeing/pooping: Place an O where Fluffy pees outside the box and an X where he poops. When you do this, think about the textures of the surface. Does he have preferences (clothes, bathtubs, newspapers)? Who they smell like?
    - Places where Fluffy likes to sleep, play and scratch

You may want to keep a journal. What happened 30 minutes before the incident? Did someone come to the door? Did the dog walk in the room? (For example: Angie's new boyfriend came over and Fluffy pissed on the couch. Fluffy peed next to the door. Fluffy peed in the corner of the room. Butch the dog is in front of the litter box. Fluffy cried out as he peed on the couch.)

If possible, set up a camera in the areas where he goes. This will help you observe something near the litter box that frightens him or uncomfortable interactions with other pets.

Questionnaire

About your cat(s)
- How much does your kitty weigh? How much does your vet say he should weigh?
    - Is your cat longhair? Medium hair? Shorthair?
    - Is kitty spayed or neutered? How old was he/she when altered?
    - Did the cat have a litter box problem when you acquired him?
    - How many cats do you have?
    - How many dogs do you have?

About the litter box
- How many litter boxes are there in the house?
- Where are the boxes located? Are they clustered together in the same room or distributed throughout the house? (Please put this on your home diagram.)
    - What type and size of litter boxes do you use? Covered box with cave-type entrance? Covered box with flap at the entrance? Modified storage box? Enclosed top entry? Large open box? Small (under 19 inches long)? Medium (20 to 22 inches long)? Large (over 30 inches long)? Electronic self-scooping box?

- How old are the boxes?
- Have you switched boxes recently?
- What kind of cat litter do you use? Scented? Unscented?
- What texture is the litter? Clumping clay? Sandy texture? Non-clumping clay? Silica gel (fine crystals)? Jagged crystals? Paper pellets? Pine pellets? Corn? Wheat? Citrus? Other?
  - Have you switched to a different litter recently?
  - What did you use before you switched?
- How often do you scoop the box? More than once a day? Once a day? Every other day? Twice a week? Once a week? Less than once a week?
- How often is the box emptied, washed and filled with fresh litter? Daily? Weekly? Every 2 weeks? Monthly? Every 2 to 3 months? Every 3 to 6 months? Never?
  - Do you use litter mats? What kind?
  - Do you use a plastic or newspaper box liner?
- Does kitty dig in his litter, or does he jump in, do his business, and quickly run away?
  - Does he stand in the box but pee or poop over the side?
  - Does he stand only on the edge of the box?
- Does your kitty *ever* pee inside the litter box? ***Ever*** poop inside the box?
  - How long ago did he start missing the box?
- How often does your kitty go outside the box? All the time? Daily? Weekly? Monthly?
  - Has it become worse recently?
- Under what circumstances does it happen (kids visiting, a stray cat is pooping in your yard)?
- Did you change anything associated with the litter box right before he began having problems?
  - What types of cleaners do you use in and around the box?
  - What kind of flooring is the box on?
- Where is he going to the bathroom (right next to the box, different locations)?
- Does your cat pee on vertical surfaces outside the litter box (walls, drapes, doors, sides of furniture, TV, cabinets, etc.)?
- Does he pee on flat surfaces outside the litter box (floor, countertops, bathtubs, furniture)?
- When he pees, does he back up to object, twitch his tail, and let loose while standing, or does he squat?
- Does your cat prefer to pee on a certain texture or material? Carpet? Clothing? Paper? Potted plants? Plastic bags? Linoleum tile, cement or

other hard surfaces? Bathtub? Or no preference; he goes everywhere?
- Do these targets have a common quality (always in a certain room, only on soft and absorbent materials, always slick surfaces)?
- When he misses the litter box, does it involve pee, poop or both?
- How often does he miss the box? All the time? Sometimes? Occasionally?
- When he pees outside the box, does he spritz a little bit or does he pee a lot?
- Does he cover pee and poop in the box?

Eating habits
- What does your cat eat (canned food, dry food, table scraps)?
- Where are your cat's food and water bowls? (Note this on the diagram.)
- When is your cat fed? Is food always available? Specific feeding times? Erratic feeding times?
- Has your kitty recently developed a voracious appetite or lost his appetite?
- Does he drink more or less than he used to?
- What kind of water bowl does he have?
- How often is the water changed?

Household
- How have you tried to correct the problem?
- How do you discipline your cat?
- Has your household changed since your cat joined the family? Death of a human? Death of another pet? Family member moved away? Marriage? New significant other? New baby? Divorce? New pet? Move to new home? Family's schedule changed (different work hours, more traveling)?
- Does your cat get along with other human family members (including boyfriends, girlfriends, grandkids and frequent visitors)?
- List all the people living at home or who visit frequently. Do they get along with the cat?
- Does he ever fight with other pets? Appear frightened by pets or people in the household?
- Do other pets or wild animals hang out in your yard?
- How does he react to outside cats?
- How long is he usually left home alone?

Health questions
- Does he strain when he pees or poops?

• Does he ever vocalize when peeing or pooping?

• Does the poop look like little balls, logs or yucky pudding?

• When did he last see the vet?

• Is he declawed? Did he have litter box problems **before** he was declawed?

• Has he been injured or suffer from physical problems?

• Does he have any medical problems (kidney disease, arthritis, diabetes)?

• What medications is he taking?

• Has your cat ever been diagnosed with urinary tract problems? When?

• Do you ever see blood in his pee or poop?

• Does he pee more often now than in the past?

I Can See Clearly Now (with a Black Light)

Crime show fans know the police use ultraviolet lights (also called UV lights, black lights or Woods lamps) to locate invisible blood stains, saliva and other bodily fluids. You're going to use it the same way, but you're primarily interested in finding cat pee.

Pick up a UV light from your favorite pet supply or janitorial supply store. I'm a big fan of the ❀Stink Free® Stink-Finder LED UV Urine Odor Detector (Stinkfree.com; 800-824-5363). It simplifies your hunt for yellow graffiti because you don't have to carry a flashlight. Novelty stores sell black lights to illuminate psychedelic posters, but they don't work worth spit on kitty crime scenes.

In a darkened room, bathed in the purple glow of a UV light, the salt in your cat's pee will glow florescent yellow regardless of how long it has been there. As you find a stain, identify it with a piece of masking tape so you can come back later and clean up with the lights on. Check every surface, horizontal and vertical: carpets, floors, baseboards, walls, windowsills, doors, drapes, countertops, tabletops and furniture.

The UV light will not only locate the pee spots, it will help you determine whether your cat is peeing or spraying. A round pattern near the litter box or other secluded places is likely pee. If the carpet, walls or baseboards glow yellow, or stains located in the middle of the floor appear in a long pattern, Fluffy is spraying. (You can learn about that in Chapter 3: Is It Peeing or Marking?)

3   IS IT PEEING OR MARKING?

Do not meddle in the affairs of cats, for they are subtle and will piss on your computer. ~Bruce Graham

If you find cat pee on your carpet, you may think it's a pretty good bet Fluffy has a litter box problem. But any good investigator knows not to jump to conclusions.

There are two primary types of kitty housesoiling: inappropriate elimination—which is a toileting issue—and spraying. Both peeing and spraying use the same bodily fluid, but they have totally distinctive functions that must be approached differently. Spraying is a cat's primary form of communication that posts essential information for other cats. It's motivated by anxiety, stress or the need to claim territory. Toileting is only about emptying the bladder. Inappropriate toileting is triggered by medical issues, anxiety, litter box aversion or bullying.

You can tell the difference between pee and spray spots by the location and shape of the stain, and the amount of pee.

Identifying a Pee Stain

Since healthy cats naturally squat to go to the bathroom, a round pee pattern delivered from a squatting position on a flat surface *usually* means Fluffy is eliminating—*but not always*. We discovered our 12-year-old calico, Eiu, was struggling with arthritis when she started peeing inside the litter box from a standing position. She could no longer squat, so she stood up and squirted pee over the top of the box onto the wall. The pattern on the wall looked exactly like a spray pattern, but a sizable puddle collected on the floor.

A peeing kitty passes a larger volume of liquid than a cat marking territory. The average kitty bladder holds 25 to 30 milliliters (around 1/8 cup). If he *never* pees in the box and he's passing the contents of a full bladder, he's eliminating.

[WARNING!] The exception is a cat suffering from a urethra blockage, in which case he'll repeatedly squat and pass just a few drops of pee, or maybe none at all. This is a medical emergency; a cat with a blockage can die within 24 hours.

Cats with elimination issues stop going inside the box altogether and instead target areas with (what they consider to be) a suitable texture. Some cats abandon their litter boxes because they don't like your choice of cat litter, box location, the type or size of box or a lack of cleanliness. A kitty who *wants* to use the litter box but finds it unacceptable may pee immediately next to it.

Urine Marking

Spraying pheromone-rich pee on vertical surfaces is one method of indirect communication in predatory and territorial animals, including cats. Pheromones are natural substances secreted by animals that leave behind chemical messages for other members of the same species.

In the *typical* marking scenario, the cat backs up to a vertical object with his tail up and wiggles his tail as he sprays a stream of pee. Both male and female cats spray from the standing position, so they can concentrate the stream at nose height for other cats to find. Males, especially unneutered males, are more likely to spray. Some kitties tread back and forth on their back feet with their eyes half-closed. There's also a faux spraying behavior, where he backs up and twitches his tail, but he's shooting blanks—no pee passes. This counterfeit behavior often happens when the cat is excited about something.

Every cat is an individual. Some cats break the rules. In some cases an offender may mark on a flat surface while squatting.

In addition to anointing the windows and furniture, a marking cat will continue to happily empty his bladder *inside* the litter box. When he marks from a standing position, he'll only spritz a little pee rather than opening the floodgates. If he's peeing inside the litter box at times, but *also* standing or squatting in the middle of your bed (or dirty clothes), he's marking rather than emptying his bladder.

Cats usually spray in socially meaningful areas, such as near windows or doors or on items that have the scent of a beloved or feared person and/or animal.

Dr. Nicholas Dodman said urine marking involves varied locations, such as new furniture, countertops, stovetops, refrigerators, shopping bags, windowsills, drapes, doors, walls, computers, personal belongings, worn clothes, or the bed of the owner, and sometimes even the people themselves. That seems to cover almost everything in your home, doesn't it? If a few of these targets have been drizzled, you can be fairly sure he's marking rather than peeing.

Dr. Dodman is the former director of the Animal Behavior Department at Tufts University Cummings School of Veterinary Medicine.

The location *and* shape of the pee stain will help you determine whether he's peeing or marking. In a darkened room using an ultraviolet light (UV or black light), cat pee appears fluorescent yellow. The black light will show you both the location and the shape of the stain (round from a squatting position or long from standing). Check the walls, baseboards, furniture, and areas around doors and windows. (Learn all about using a black light in I Can See Clearly Now (with a Black Light) in Chapter 2.)

Is It Pee or Graffiti?

He's peeing if:	He's marking if:
Cat *never* pees inside the litter box, but usually goes *near the box*	Cat *continues* to pee inside the box several times a day *and* sprays other places such as furniture, your bed, your dirty clothes, and near doors and windows
Produces large volume of pee when he empties his bladder	Sprays small quantity of pee
Usually scratches to cover	Doesn't attempt to cover
Sniffs the area after going	Sniffs area before going, but not after
	Backs up to a vertical object wiggling his tail, spraying urine, and wearing a euphoric expression

Squats near the litter box	Dances side to side on back feet
Squats, making a round pattern; this is *usually* peeing (but not always)	*Stands* in the middle of a flat surface, producing a long stream
Usually goes on flat surfaces	Often goes on vertical surfaces such as walls, doors and furniture arms
Usually in a discreet place	On varied places around the home, and on personal items
In the middle of the room he squats, peeing large volumes	When he marks the middle of the room, he leaves only a small volume of pee

Stephanie

4 WHODUNIT? APPREHENDING THE SUSPECT(S) IN A MULTIPET HOME

No matter what the cat has done wrong, she will always try to make it look as if the dog did it. ~Unknown

When you have only one pet, you *know* who peed on the carpet. But add a kitty companion or a couple of dogs and you suddenly have to become a pet detective to determine who's turning on the sprinkler.

When investigating "litter box" problems in a multipet home, keep an open mind. You might think it's the "angry" or "bossy" cat, or you might rule out the dog because he goes when you take him outside. A good detective must rule out the prime suspects, as well as seemingly innocent bystanders. Consider conspiracies involving multiple perps, or coercion of the fearful. These same dynamics occur in multipet homes. The more suspects, the harder it is to pin the culprit.

Observation

Even if you actually witness a yellow paint vandal committing the crime, you can't disqualify other conspirators. They might be better at not getting caught. When one pet pees on the carpet, often others join him.

Cats are such creatures of habits, so deviations in their everyday patterns may signal something's wrong. Monitor changes in behavior or routine. If you notice any new or odd behaviors, take kitty to the vet.

Round Up the Usual Suspects

Whenever a litter box problem first rears its ugly rear, one at a time, sequester past litter box offenders in a bathroom or small room. He'll only stay segregated until he goes to the bathroom; certainly no more than 24 hours. This is not prison time, so make sure the cat has someplace warm and snuggly to sleep, toys, water, food, attention from you, and a clean litter box (placed away from his food and water). If he misses his box while he's separated, you'll know he's a confirmed accomplice. But just because he doesn't miss the box in seclusion doesn't dismiss him as a suspect. Removing a cat from the environment may change the social dynamics and alter his bathroom behavior.

Marking Bodily Fluids

You may have to resort to marking your cats' secretions the way a bank teller uses dye packets to mark bills inside a bag of stolen money. Cat pee, under normal circumstances, glows yellow-green when viewed in a darkened room under an ultraviolet light. This makes pee spots in the carpet a cinch to locate. The problem is, the ultraviolet light tells you where the spots are, but not who left them.

Your vet can mark a pet's pee using fluorescein, a medical solution ophthalmologists use to diagnose eye injuries. Fluorescein leaves a harmless tracer in the cat's pee. Under a UV light, fluorescein-infused pee lights up bright apple green like a psychedelic poster.

Give the solution orally to one cat at a time daily for three days, or ask your vet to give your cat an injection of fluorescein. ⚠This may not be a good option if you have a light-colored carpet or furniture. Both oral and injectable fluorescein can permanently stain the carpet and upholstery. To be safe, color test your carpet in an out-of-the-way corner with undigested fluorescein and water.

Once the cat's pee has been "tagged" with fluorescein, look inside the litter box with the black light. If the kitty still uses the box, a bright glow should appear among the litter. Is he peeing in the box, but also on the walls? That means he's eliminating in the box but marking in other locations. Is the litter box devoid of fluorescein? He's avoiding his litter box and has found another place to go to the bathroom. Day glow spots found on a vertical object means he's spraying. Check the walls, baseboards, furniture, windows and doors.

Because fluorescein only comes in one color, you can't test more than one kitty at a time. You'll have to wait 24 hours to allow the chemical to dissipate from Fluffy's system before treating the next cat. Finally, if the kitty only pees outside the box sporadically, fluorescein may not catch the cat in the act.

Whose Poop Is It?

Dr. Cynthia Rigoni, owner of All Cats Veterinary Hospital in Houston, said you can identify the depositor of inappropriate poop by feeding your entire feline family *finely chopped* rubber bands. Quarter-inch pieces will pass through Fluffy's GI tract without being digested or harming the cat, resulting in colorful confetti turds that reveal just who's pooping and where. Add one-half teaspoon to canned food, baby food or tuna. Keep a log of who gets which color: Fluffy gets green, Tabby gets yellow, and Max gets blue.

You can also accomplish the same thing by feeding the kitties shavings of *nontoxic* crayons with something yummy. Shred the crayons with a cheese grater. When you find the runny poop or puke loaded with green band bits or crayon shreds, you'll know that DooVinci needs to go to the vet.

Video Surveillance

Just like the television crime shows, you may want to set up video surveillance to catch your culprits. You can invest in an inexpensive motion-triggered video device or trail camera, and set it up by the latest spray area. Infrared allows you to monitor unauthorized eliminations at night—hunters use them to track wildlife movement. Point the camera at hot spots while you're working or sleeping. When you return, you can see everyone who's anointing the rug.

Unless your cats have predictable targets, you need to arrange cameras throughout the house. Fortunately, cameras are very affordable these days. Don't stop when you nab your first suspect. You might be surprised how many offenders are participating.

"Busted!"

5 CAUGHT IN THE ACT

If you yell at a cat, you're the one who is making a fool of yourself. ~
Unknown

Oh no! Fluffy's squatting in the corner of the living room again. Your first instinct may be to yell, "Bad kitty!" and swat his butt. But "bad" is all a matter of perspective, isn't it? In the cat's mind, what he did was necessary, and the screaming human is freakin' nuts.

Crime and Punishment

Punishment is an action intended to decrease the recurrence of an unwanted behavior. When caught and convicted, human criminals go to jail. Hopefully, the fear of incarceration will deter them from becoming repeat offenders. We punish kitties with the same intent.

But, there's a problem. Humans can look back and think, "Maybe robbing that convenience store wasn't worth five years in prison." But cats live in the present—right in this instant. They don't mentally go back in time like we do, not even a few seconds. So Fluffy doesn't connect that swat to the butt with peeing on the carpet two minutes ago.

Noted veterinary behaviorist Dr. Andrew U. Luescher, said in "Compulsive Behavior in Companion Animals," "If the animal is to associate punishment with the undesirable action, it has to be delivered *every time the behavior is performed*, immediately after the behavior is performed, and at the right intensity." According to Dr. Luescher, the timing of punishment must occur "within .5 seconds of the start of the behavior. A delay of a few seconds makes punishment ineffective. Punishment must follow the behavior *every time*, must never occur without the behavior, and should not be related to the handler." If punishment is effective, it works within three or four times.

Because you can't watch your kitty 24/7, it's impossible to effectively punish him. To Fluffy, physical discipline is unpredictable. That hand or scream comes out of the blue. Imagine how stressful it would be to never know when the hand of God is going to strike out at you.

Dr. L said punishment doesn't teach appropriate behavior, but it does increase anxiety. It actually inhibits learning and exacerbates behavior problems. It also affects the human-animal bond.

If you yank Fluffy up while he's peeing on the floor, then throw him in the litter box, he'll make a negative association *with the box* rather than a positive one. In fact, lunatic behavior (in Fluffy's eyes) will intensify his stress and he'll associate punishment with the actual act of going to the bathroom, not going in the wrong place. Now he's scared of the box *and* having to pee *and* you. So he'll just wait until he's alone to relieve himself. The added anxiety level will stress him into urine marking (even more). And thus begins the vicious cycle of crime and punishment that can't have a good ending. Trust is broken on both sides. Everybody loses.

Just because you abolish corporal punishment doesn't mean you have to tolerate soggy carpets. Research has shown that reinforcing a good behavior is more effective than punishing unwanted behavior. Think long term. Make his preferred spot unattractive to him (Making Inappropriate Elimination Unpleasant in Chapter 15 explains how to do this), offer him an acceptable alternative, and praise him when he goes in an appropriate place. Everyone gets what they want.

Because inappropriate elimination often starts with a medical condition, instead of punishing Fluffy, take him to the vet.

"Regardless of the cause, try to keep calm," Dr. Tony Buffington said.

"Our cats need reassurance that all is well; our calmness signals safety." Dr. Buffington is a retired professor from Ohio State University College of Veterinary Medicine, and author of the *Indoor Cat Initiative* (IndoorPet.osu.edu/cats) and *Cat Mastery*. He is now a full-time evangelist for effective environmental enrichment for cats.

So what do you do? I'll get into that a lot more as the book goes on, but here's the short answer: Give your cat what he wants and needs.

If your kitty has had a frightening or painful litter box experience, offer him a completely different style of box with unique qualities. Fill it with a different type of unscented litter and set it up in a new location. An entirely different toilet setup may help him overcome his negative association with the box.

If the cat is being bullied by another pet, he will benefit from an environment of plenty—litter boxes in several different parts of the home—because a bully can't guard all the boxes at the same time. (I cover that in Chapter 9 Hurry Up in There! Potty Issues in the Multipet Home and Chapter 13 Environmental Enrichment: Just What the Doctor Ordered.)

So let's make sure from now on Fluffy's litter box experience is what he wants:

- Pain-free potty opportunities
- A cleaner litter box
- A bigger or open litter box
- Unscented litter
- A softer litter texture
- More litter boxes
- A quieter location
- Protection from bullies

Whenever you catch your kitty scratching inside the litter box, go into the room, and from the door in your happiest praise voice say, "What a good boy!" Do it from a distance. Don't stand over him. If you have a treat handy, toss it to him when he's finished his business.

What to Do When You Catch Him in the Act

There are three schools of thought about how people should react when walking in on a kitty mid-sprinkle.

1.   Stay calm. If he's peeing within a few feet of a litter box, say something in a sweet, high-pitched voice like, "Whoops." If you can do it in a totally calm way, gently pick him up, scooping his tail under him so he doesn't squirt. Quickly and *gently*, set him in the litter box. End with a sincere, "Good boy." You want him to associate good feelings with the act

of eliminating and being in the box. The next step is to draw up a plan to provide him with an acceptable bathroom. (This is the method I prefer.)

2.   Stay calm. Don't react vocally at all. At your earliest opportunity, figure out what's bothering him and fix it. Keep reading. You'll figure it out.

3.   Stay calm. If he's spraying or preparing to mark, interrupt the action. In a high, nonconfrontational voice (translate to mean sweet), say, "Whoop, whoop, whoop!" or "Hey, what are you doing?" Pick him up and *gently* place him in the litter box. Say, "Good boy" and walk away.

The time to react is *before* he opens the floodgates, as he's positioning himself to pee or when he's backing up to his target to spray, not during or after.

No need to scream, because cats have Superman hearing. "Dude, whatcha doing?" After you get the cat's attention, put him into the box as a gentle reminder. Do this whenever you see his peeing prelude.

Dr. L said there are alternatives to punishment.

• **Do not reward**

• **Reduce Fluffy's motivation for spraying or going outside the box** (Chapter 15 Litter Box Rehab discusses this.)

• **Provide an acceptable alternative** (Learn about this in Chapter 8 Cat Tagging: When Kitty Marks, Chapter 6 Thinking Inside the Litter Box and Chapter 15 Litter Box Rehab.)

• **Systematic desensitization**. This exposes a cat to whatever upsets him, but in such small amounts that it doesn't provoke a reaction. You gradually increase the intensity of the exposure until your cat can experience the trigger without reacting.

• **Counterconditioning.** This teaches the cat to accept something he doesn't like (trimming toenails, taking pills or being around a cat he doesn't like) by associating it with something he wants (his favorite treat.)

A study by Dr. B.L. Hart, professor emeritus of veterinary anatomy, physiology, and cell biology and director of the Center for Animal Behavior at the UC Davis College of Biological Sciences, found that the frequency of spraying was reduced when owners didn't punish the cat, gave the kitty treats every day, and provided an ideal litter box. Although the study was on spraying, this technique should improve litter box compliance as well. A calm environment and snacks help Fluffy associate something positive with his owner, and reduce stress. Simply providing an acceptable litter box can also reduce stress and spraying.

"I guess humans don't like covered boxes either."

6 THINKING INSIDE THE LITTER BOX

Cats didn't evolve to pee in plastic caves filled with man-made litter placed in locations selected by another species.
~Sharon L. Crowell-Davis, DVM, PhD, DACVB

Thousands of years ago, the Egyptians worshipped cats as gods. Back in the day, the kitties enjoyed a perpetually clean, unscented sand box as big as the Sinai itself, a toilet worthy of a god.

Because of their natural inclination to eliminate in loose material and cover their waste, cats have become the most popular four-legged pet in

23

the United States. But honestly, they don't do it that way to please you. This tidy nature has a life and death origin, said Dr. Tony Buffington. "Small cats in nature are both predators and prey species, so they generally eliminate in safe, private places to avoid announcing their presence to predators during these vulnerable moments."

Humans and the Restroom

Ask yourself, what do *you* expect when you use a public restroom? You'll likely say a civilized toilet should be clean, with no residual waste, no foul odors, and enough room to perform the task at hand. Nobody wants to go into those filthy fairground portable toilets with many different forms of DNA coating the toilet seat and walls and barely enough room to do what you're there for.

Even in your own home you probably have bathroom expectations. With the exception of those on septic systems, you probably expect people to flush the commode after every use. After all, no one wants to see someone else's poop in the toilet.

Then, there's the other end of the Yuck Scale. "Have you ever been in an airport and the housekeepers have overdone the disinfectants and air freshener?" Beth Adelman, CCBC, a cat behavior consultant in Brooklyn, asks. "We feel like choking. Cats do too."

So let's review what *you* want in a bathroom: a spacious, clean, odor-free area with flushed toilets. Great! This is one thing both you and your cat agree on. However, we often expect fastidious Fluffy to use bathroom facilities we'd be appalled by.

In many homes the cat's toilet has been relegated to a 12-inch by 18-inch plastic cave hidden in the basement behind a sign that warns, "Beware the Leopard." Not only does this poor kitty have to avoid an obstacle course of poop and pee, he must hold his breath inside the box because the combination of ammonia, old waste and floral-scented litter makes the air unbreathable. Then we blame the cat for choosing a better place to go. Really, is that fair?

Your cat's preferences are important. Just give Fluffy what he wants, and he will give you what you want.

What Makes a Great Litter Box?

It depends on who's answering the question. If I asked you to list everything you want in a litter box, I bet some of the things you'd mention include:
- Scoops itself or is easy to scoop
- Keeps odor contained

- Doesn't take up much room
- Has a pleasant fragrance
- Doesn't track litter
- Ecologically friendly
- Inexpensive
- Attractive or you don't have to look at it

Your cat's Wish List is much shorter. Fluffy basically wants the Sahara Desert—a vast, safe, convenient area filled with clean, soft sand that doesn't smell. That's all. No bells or whistles.

Does He Like His Box?

Because of their desert heritage, cats are hardwired for certain litter box preferences. The worst thing you can do is to give your cat a reason *not* to use the litter box. People do it all the time. While appealing to our human need for convenience, people unintentionally give cats countless reasons to avoid their designated restroom.

"In general, owner-related reasons are the number one cause of house-soiling," said Carlo Siracusa, DVM, MS, PhD, Diplomate of the American College of Veterinary Behaviorists, chief of the animal behavior service and of the Primary Care Education Section at the School of Veterinary Medicine of the University of Pennsylvania. However, "Among behavior problems, housesoiling is the problem with the best prognosis if the owner is educated."

Does Fluffy Like His Box?

Watch Fluffy when he uses his box. Does he jump out immediately or shake his paws or dash away as if running from a vet wielding a rectal thermometer? If you observe these reluctant behaviors, your cat is sending you a very clear message: He doesn't like his toilet.

A healthy cat should enjoy the litter box process. He should sniff around to find just the right place to go, dig, linger, dig some more and cover.

The most common reasons cats avoid the litter box include:
- Medical issues (take kitty to the vet)
- Too dirty
- Box too small
- Hooded box
- Doesn't like the litter
- Poor location
- Box cleaned with strong-smelling chemicals
- Not enough boxes
- Presence of litter box liners or litter mat

- Litter depth too shallow
- Another pet (or kid) is guarding the litter box
- Getting into the box is painful

Pay attention to Fluffy when he misses the box. If he only goes outside the box when it hasn't been scooped, he wants a cleaner box. If he started peeing outside the box after you bought a new type of litter, a new box, or moved the box to a new spot, he's telling you he doesn't like the change.

Tails from the Trenches

Beth Adelman had a client whose cat, Henry, was going outside the box. When asked which litter she was using, the client said she'd tried many different cat litters before finding "one the cat liked." Using the Goldilocks preference method, the first brand she had tried tracked too much, and the second left little paw prints around the house; the grains of the third brand were big and scratched the floor. Finally she found the current litter, which she assured Beth the cat liked because it didn't track and it had a nice cedar scent. None of the traits the client listed were important to the cat. They were only important to the owner.

"That tells me why *you* like the litter," Adelman told her client. "It doesn't tell me why *the cat* likes the litter."

The client liked to cook, so Adelman set up a scenario the woman could relate to. "Imagine you have a roommate who saw a picture in a magazine and said, 'I'm going to redo the kitchen like the magazine.'" The roommate, who doesn't cook, places the appliances and cooking utensils where they look good, not where they are most convenient for cooking.

"That's like what happens when you ignore what the cat wants," Adelman explained. "The cat may have preferences for a certain litter or litter box, based on past experience. Likewise, the cat may *dislike* a certain kind of box or litter based on past experience."

The woman "got it," and switched to a litter the cat really did like. The cat started using the litter box again. Happy ending.

Cleanliness Is Next to Catliness

Human parents know when a baby needs to be changed by The Smell. They don't pin rose-scented diapers on the tyke and change him only after he leaves tread marks on the carpet. When the bouquet of baby poop wafts from the direction of the infant, parents bring out butt wipes and fresh diapers and clean him up.

It's the same with scented litter versus cat pee. No matter how much you want to cover it up, perfume doesn't stop ammonia from smelling like ammonia. If you need fragrance to cover the box smell, just clean the box.

Think about this: You go into a gas station restroom. The first stall has a toilet that wasn't flushed by the last person. Disgusting! You need only press the handle to get a clean toilet, yet most people will quickly exit and go to another stall. It's the same with your cat—except he doesn't have the option to flush the box himself. If his restroom is too vile, he too will seek out another option.

Ignore the litter box at your carpet's risk. To rephrase a popular proverb, "Neglect in haste, mop pee at leisure."

"I tell people, if you scoop twice a day, it's not a big chore," Adelman said. "It takes 15 seconds. That's all. It's a bigger chore if you wait, plus poop stinks. Why would you want to have that smell around? You don't like it; the cat doesn't like it. You can spend a lot of money on air freshener or you can clean the box when the cat uses it. At least twice a day, plus whenever you see or smell something."

"Would you like to step into poop in order to use the bathroom?" asks Jacqueline Munera, CCBC, PCBC, CAP 2 and cat behavior consultant from Tampa, FL. "Your cat doesn't either." Just as women in a nasty gas station bathroom assume the most outrageous positions to avoid contact with the toilet seat, the cat has to contort into an uncomfortable stance rather than risk contact with an equally nasty litter box, Munera said.

Munera has observed the cats of clients carefully balance all four paws on the walls of the litter box so they don't have to touch the disgusting minefield below. While technically the cat is standing in the box, his poop drops over the side onto the floor. Fluffy gets an "A" for effort. The owner gets an "F" for failure to scoop.

Munera has been known to ask clients to stick their heads inside the covered litter box so they can see and smell exactly what the cat experiences. "They come out with their eyes wide. They finally understand why the cat doesn't want to go in the box. The cleaner the box is, the more likely the cat is to use it."

She also reminds her germ-conscious clients that when the cat walks inside a dirty litter box, he steps on poop and then walks all over the house.

In addition to making the cat happy, there are financial incentives to scoop frequently. If you scoop promptly after Fluffy goes, the remaining litter won't have time to absorb odors, saving you money on cat litter (and deodorizers).

Many behaviorists recommend tossing used litter every week and washing the box with diluted bleach. Dr. Dodman prefers cleaning the box with warm running water only, as a slight residual odor may help attract the cat to the box. How often your cat's box needs to be changed depends on how many boxes you have, how often you scoop, how many cats you have, how popular that particular box is, what kind of litter you use and whether the pee clumps break apart.

Adelman recommends odor testing the litter every time you scoop. Get a couple of inches away from the litter surface (about cat nose height), and take a sniff. If the scooped litter smells musty or you detect ammonia, it's time to wash the box and fill it with clean litter.

And if after cleaning the box, the house still has The Smell, it's time to check the floor, walls and furniture. (Chapter 7 Crime Scene Cleanup will show you how to get the smell of cat pee out of carpet and furniture.)

If you use non-clumping litters, scoop the poop *and* wet spots no less than twice a day, and dump the litter and wash the box at least a couple of times a week. As with clumping litter, take a sniff after you scoop. If it smells, it's time to throw out the old litter and wash the box.

Regardless of your regular cleaning schedule, change traditional litter whenever the litter looks wet and soggy; litter should look and feel dry.

How to Scoop a Litter Box

When scooping, avoid breaking pee clumps apart. This can be a problem if you use a light, flexible plastic scoop. If you can't feel the pee clump, it's easy to fracture it. Ammonia-soaked fragments drop back into the box, contaminating the unused litter. Pee clumps may also cling to the walls and corners of the box, breaking apart when you scoop. My favorite litter scoop is the ✿Litter-Lifter® (Preferred Merchandizing, Inc.; Litter-Lifter.com; 888-548-8375), a rigid, but comfortable scoop that makes fast work of litter boxes without breaking clumps apart.

Dr. Buffington said the litter needs to be deep enough (2 to 3 inches) so the cat's paws don't hit the bottom of the box when he digs. That depth also allows the clump to float on top of loose litter.

If the litter is deep enough, you should be able to give the box a couple of vigorous shakes, and clumps will drift to the surface. You can then run your scoop well beneath each clump, plucking it up intact.

Spraying the clean, empty box floor and walls with aerosol cooking spray prevents sticking. Any pee clumps stuck to the walls can be dislodged with a firm bump to the outside of the box, so you can scoop them from beneath.

Wipe the box sides with a damp paper towel. If you use a covered box, hose off the inside of the hood.

A Box Worthy of a God

Although covering their waste is a natural feline behavior, the litter box is purely a human invention. The small tray we typically provide is nothing like the open area cats evolved to go in. While there's no 100 percent litter box rule that applies to every cat, cats generally prefer large, uncovered litter boxes.

"One of the most common mistakes owners make is litter boxes tend to be very small," Dr. Siracusa said.

When buying a new litter box, think big—big as the great desert of Egypt. Okay, maybe not *that* big, but your cat should be able to stand up on all fours and turn around in the box. Anything smaller makes it difficult for him to cover his poop. At the very minimum, the box should measure 1½ times the length of the cat from the nose to the tip of the tail. Dr. Siracusa went a step further: "Twice the length of the cat is ideal."

Even the largest commercially available litter box isn't large enough for the typical 8- to 15-pound housecat, Dr. Sharon Crowell-Davis said in her proceeding, "Educating Clients to Prevent Feline Behavioral Problems" at the North American Veterinary Conference in 2005. "Offering these to your cat is like offering a toddler's training potty to your houseguests."

Compared to the bathroom rituals of outside cats, kitties using standard-size litter boxes are obviously cramped.

"Cats like to stretch. If she can't do this (in the box), she'll go somewhere else," Siracusa said. "The rug may do the job." Not only is the rug open, he reminds us, "it absorbs the pee as any good sand would."

Offer your cat a large plastic storage box, such as an under-bed sweater storage bin, litter pans designed for small dogs, or if you have room, a plastic kid's wading pool would give large cats plenty of room to work.

The only name brand litter box I recommend is the ❧Petmate Giant Litter Pan (pictured on pg 31) (Petmate.com; 877-738-6283.) While it's not pretty, it has everything a cat wants in a bathroom. It's open and roomy. I also like the ❧Ace Hardware 36-inch x 24-inch 23-gallon Super Tub #1522929.

"My rule is if the cat has all four feet in the box, he gets credit for being in the box," Beth Adelman said. "So if stuff lands outside the box, *you* have to make the change, not the cat."

When choosing a litter box, consider your cat's physique and condition. A large Maine Coon needs a bigger bathroom than a lithe Siamese. Although bigger is usually better, remember kittens, senior cats and cats suffering from illness, arthritis or disabilities may need a box with lower entry for easy access.

Figure 1 - Beth Adelman made a large, easy to enter box from a large storage container. Photo by Beth Adelman.

If you use clumping litter, don't buy a box with sharp corners or floor grooves. When using non-clumping litter, the channels collect pee. When clumps form inside the channel, it's almost impossible to remove them without fracturing the clump. Rounded corners and flat floors will prolong the life of the litter and cut down on odors.

Tails from the Trenches

Lauren-Ashley Oliver has a 15-year-old white kitty named Rufus who started going right outside the litter box.

"We eventually realized that he wasn't getting in the box far enough. The sides were too short and he was just spilling out over the edge and sides."

She added a larger, top entry litter box and cut a front entrance in it. She also placed wee-wee pads around and under the small litter box. Problem solved.

Trouble in the Hood-ed Box

Nobody wants to go inside that fairground potty in a box. If you're a plus size, like Queen Latifah or Dwayne "The Rock" Johnson, there's no way that shoebox of a bathroom is acceptable. I'd also be willing to bet your cat feels the same way about his covered litter box.

In nature, cats go to a secluded but open area with an easy escape. Cats don't climb inside a narrow cave or hollowed-out log to poop because they'd be vulnerable. If a coyote approaches when the cat is mid-squat inside a crevasse, he has nowhere to go. He's breakfast.

While some cats deign to use hooded boxes, many avoid them. Like the hollow log, covered boxes can be downright scary. In multicat homes, the view is obscured from both inside and outside. The cat inside the box may fear an unseen bully waiting to pounce. Because they have only one exit, it's easy for a cat to be trapped inside by the bully cat, an annoying dog or the 4-year old neighbor brat. No kitty in his right mind is going to go back for more of that. Even worse are the enclosed boxes with the entry hole on top. Older cats may have a hard time getting in.

Covered litter boxes trap odors inside. Unless they are kept squeaky clean, they provide kitties with the same nose-searing experience as your last trip to the fairground toilet. Although many families use hooded boxes to keep the dog from Tootsie Roll® grazing, that could backfire because the cat may fear the covered box itself.

Figure 2 - Sam shows off the size of the Petmate® Giant Litter Pan. While not quite one-and-a-half times the cat's length, it is one of the few commercially available litter boxes that gives the cat room to move around.
Photo by Weems S. Hutto.

Covered boxes are a problem especially for large cats. Big boys and girls don't have room to move around and cover their waste. That's why you often see cats scratching outside the box.

If your cat is avoiding his enclosed box, just take the top off or cut a second opening in the hood, and scoop the box at least twice a day. The problem is often solved that easily. Give your cat a side-by-side choice between enclosed and open boxes. He'll show you which one he wants.

Make a More Acceptable Covered Box

Jennifer Mauger, a certified dog trainer and cat behaviorist from Akron, Ohio, said "If you need a covered box to keep a dog out or keep litter inside the box, then make your own out of a large, clear storage container."

The base measurement should be at least 18 inches by 22 inches and tall enough for the cat inside to stand up normally. (The label will list the size.) Cut two holes for both an entrance and exit. Using a hair dryer, heat up the side of the box where you are going to place the first hole. The heat will allow you to cut it easily. Make sure the hole is at least 6 inches from the bottom, unless your cat suffers from mobility problems. Using a utility knife, cut a hole. Repeat with a second hole on the other side. Finish by either sanding the entrance edges smooth or covering them with duct tape.

Self-Scooping Boxes

Self-scooping electronic boxes might be modern marvels that reduce the need for scooping, but they may also send a nervous kitty running for the hills. Some cats love them; some cats hate them. Automatic litter boxes can be terrifying if a shy or fearful cat walks up as the machine begins its cleaning cycle. Also, because the motors take up so much space, they don't give the kitty much working room.

On the plus side, electronic boxes may make it possible for elderly or disabled people to care for a cat. If this is the case, leave the device off and activate the rake only when the cat is out of the room.

Toilet Training Systems

Toilet training kit for cats—this is another one of those, "It seemed like a good idea at the time" concepts. It's supposed to be a panacea—no more litter boxes—but it's a bad idea on so many levels. Cats have the need to dig and bury their waste. This deprives them of that possibility.

Even if you can train your cat to use the toilet, you may still have to deal with inappropriate elimination issues as Fluffy ages. An older cat with arthritis may not be able to jump up or balance on the seat without pain. In his later years, you will have to provide him with a ramp or steps so he can access his toilet. Do you really want to make an arthritic cat climb stairs just to pee?

Tails from the Trenches

I admit in the 1980s I tried to teach my first cat, Houston, to use a toilet. The plastic training unit collapsed and Houston fell into the commode. After that, he wouldn't even enter the bathroom where his litter box had been. By trying to train him to do something unnatural, I wound up creating a problem where one didn't exist.

Later, I interviewed a woman who successfully trained her cat to use the toilet without fail. However, she said cats are not discriminating about how they position themselves on the commode seat. Every time he went to the bathroom, he peed on the seat and down the side of the toilet bowl. Since she couldn't untrain him, she gave him "his" restroom. She told me she wouldn't be able to reclaim her guest bathroom until her cat died.

Also, when your cat eliminates into a toilet, you lose the ability to monitor health problems. You won't know how frequently he's peeing or whether it contains blood.

Personally, I'd rather scoop the box than sanitize the toilet seat every night.

Cat Litter that's Worth a Piss

Scanning the cat litter aisles of your pet supplier, you'll see more than 100 different brands and styles of cat litter flaunting additives that smell flowery, control odors, attract cats and even diagnose illnesses. Cat litter can clump, flush, compost and even provide tire traction on icy driveways. In choosing a litter for your cat, you'll consider a number of factors: convenience, expense, odor control and other desirable extras. With all those options, *your cat's* litter druthers boil down to only two factors: scratch and sniff.

While litter preferences may vary, studies show that most cats prefer a cat litter similar to what their Egyptian ancestors peed in—soft, unscented sand. Since it's not cost-effective to import sand from the Sinai, you need to provide him with an acceptable substitute.

The problem with scented litter

According to veterinary behaviorist, Nicholas Dodman, scented litter is one of the most common reasons cats avoid the box.

Manufacturers add fragrance to appeal to nasally challenged humans, not for the cats who must use the litter. To keep Fluffy happily using his box, approach cat litter through the mind of a cat.

Turns out, scented litter (as well as nearby air fresheners and strong-smelling cleaning products) can make a very effective cat repellent.

Tails from the Trenches

Dr. Tony Buffington was visiting friends when the wife mentioned her black cat, Sophie, didn't like to use the litter box. Sophie's box contained a highly scented litter the woman really liked. Dr. B suggested that she set up a second litter box adjacent to the original, filled with a finer-textured, unscented litter. Despite loving the strong fragrance of the litter in her bathroom, she reluctantly followed his instructions. Sophie immediately began ignoring her old box and exclusively using the unscented litter, with no further accidents.

The Rainbolt Test Kitties and I have conducted informal litter preference tests for different magazines and litter companies since 1999. When it comes to scented litters, my product testers have consistently shown me the bolder the fragrance, the more likely they are to avoid it. They also showed a preference for low-dust litters.

Citrus in the litter box

We all want to do the right thing for the environment. And what's more environmentally responsible than using renewable, compostable material in your cat's litter box? Several years ago a citrus peel cat litter appeared on the market. Using byproducts from the citrus industry seems like a great idea. After all, orange and lemon make refreshing toilet bowl cleaners. But to your kitty, it's as disgusting as a skunk-scented air freshener.

I tested the citrus litter against other litters, and just one brave Test Kitty tried it—once. Not only did the Test Kitties avoid the box with the citrus litter, they didn't use the box next to it either. The Kitties' response wasn't surprising, because citrus is the active ingredient in many natural cat repellents.

The citrus peel cat litter only stayed on the market for a year before going the way of the sabre tooth cat. But citrus litter products continue to show up from time to time. Just today I found a citrus litter box odor eliminating additive at Walmart. Of course, it's going to eliminate litter box odors. The cat isn't going to use a box with citrus in it.

Once again, these products were formulated to make people feel good. Neither the manufacturer, the store, nor the owners who bought the stuff gave any consideration about whether or not citrus in the litter box was good for the cat. I shudder to think how many cats were surrendered to shelters because they avoided cat repellent in their boxes.

Litter textures: soft as a kitten's butt

Heavily perfumed litters aren't the only litter quality that can send kitties to sniff out the carpet. Cats can be very sensitive to texture. Walking on large grained or pelleted litters is the human equivalent of walking on large gravel barefoot. It's uncomfortable.

"Most cats prefer a soft, fine-grained clumping litter," veterinary researcher Dr. Buffington said.

We're back to Egypt again. (The exception is longhaired cats with fluffy paw tufts. See the next page.)

The uneven texture of pelleted litter, huge jagged crystals and large-grained litters may not seem like that big a deal to you, but your cat may find walking on them darned uncomfortable, maybe even painful. That's not even in the same continent as the desert sand your cat's ancestors once peed in. Fluffy evolved to use sand and dirt, and that's what your kitty likely prefers.

Why does texture matter? Imagine you're on a camping trip. The bathroom is spacious and clean, no odor, but you must stand barefooted on sharp-edged crushed stone to use the toilet. You may find it painful. As with the filthy gas station restroom, you might be tempted to seek out a nearby tree rather than endure rocks against your feet.

Next trip, the bathrooms have been renovated. The crushed stone has been replaced by soft cool sand. You linger because the sand feels good against your bare skin. You might even draw pictures in the sand with your toes or stop to build a sandcastle. Super fun.

In preference tests, cats choose fine-grained litters over larger textures, just as you would choose to walk barefoot over sand rather than crushed rocks.

To get a better feline perspective, place your inner forearm in clean litter and press down. If it feels soft and velvety next to your skin, you should have a happy cat. If it's scratchy or uncomfortable, Fluffy's probably feeling your pain.

When asked about scented or rocky litters, owners often say, "It's okay. He uses it." He may use it today, but that doesn't mean he'll continue to tolerate it in the future. If he becomes sick or stressed, the marginal litter may no longer be bearable.

Because I have a multicat home, I offer the Rainbolt Test Kitties a variety of textures and materials to accommodate different litter preferences. I do have a few cats that like wood litter. Instead of offering the uncomfortable pellets, after I place new pellets in the box, I add several cups of water that break them down into sawdust. It does the trick, and the Test Kitties appreciate it.

The hard-working testers have shown a decisive preference for ❧Dr. Elsey's® Cat Attract and ❧Precious Cat Senior (both litters come from PreciousCat.com; 877-311-2287), which is formulated for senior, arthritic, overweight, pregnant or post-operative cats. For people who feel the need to use renewable/biodegradable/flushable litter, the Test Kitties also like ❧World's Best Cat Litter Advanced Natural Pine Blend (WorldsBestCatLitter.com; 877-367-9225) and ❧ CatSpot™ Litter, which is a nonclumping litter made exclusively of finely ground coconut husk byproduct (Midwest Organics CatSpotLitter.com; 844-624-3125.) CatSpot feels and smells like natural dirt.

Veterinary behaviorist Carlo Siracusa said some cats prefer softer litters for peeing and harder litters for pooping. Offer these cats two side-by-side boxes.

Longhaired Cats and Clumping Litter

Research studies and anecdotal evidence suggests longhaired cats, especially Persians and Himalayans, have special litter box issues. While most cats like fine, unscented clumping litter, that's not true of longhaired cats with dense paw tufts. Wet clumps can cling to toe pad fur tufts. As kitties walk around, the dried, hard clumps tug, causing pain with every step.

Longhaired kitties are also more prone to ending up with pee and poop clinging to their long bloomers. Talk to your vet or groomer about a sanitary trim, which shortens the fur beneath the tail and down the back of the legs. This will prevent the long bloomers from getting soiled or matted during elimination.

If you have a longhaired kitty with litter box issues, try a nonclumping litter like ❧CatSpot™ Litter, ❧Precious Cat Long Haired Cat Litter or ❧ Precious Cat Senior litter (Preciouscat.com; 877-311-2287.) These silica gel litters won't adhere to the toe tufts. The crystals are also infused with Dr. Elsey's herbal attractant.

Tails from the Trenches

Kim Nestor, a California-based cat behaviorist at the Pasadena Humane Society and SPCA, had a client with a silver tabby named Audrey, who started going outside a pine pellet-filled litter box. Nestor prescribed an unscented, fine-textured clumping litter and scooping twice a day. In less than a week the client called with the great news that Audrey was back on track.

Texture and declawed cats

A soft texture is especially important for declawed cats, as their feet may be more sensitive than a cat whose toes are intact. If your cat is declawed, comfortable texture is all the more critical. (Learn about declawing difficulties in Chapter 11's Declawed Cats.)

Rainbolt Test Kitties' favorite litters: Precious Cat Box fillers

Many of the experts interviewed for this book recommended ❧Dr. Elsey's (Precious Cat) litters, especially for cats who show litter box reluctance.

They are formulated to make cats *want* to use it. Although they're not perfumed, they're spiked with a proprietary herbal attractant that most cats find irresistible. ❧Senior Attract, a fine-grained silica gel litter, is the Test Cats' all-time favorite cat litter. It was very effective in monitoring Cosmo, who suffered from frequent bouts of bloody pee caused by feline idiopathic cystitis. The attractant tempted him back to the box after quite a long hiatus. Because of the soft, sandy texture, it's also a great choice for declawed kitties or any cat with paw sensitivity. In my unscientific tests, Senior Attract litter received more use than any litter in the house.

"Get Dr. Elsey's Cat Attract, especially for cats who show litter box reluctance," Mieshelle Nagelschneider said. She is a cat behaviorist at The Cat Behavior Clinic in Portland, Ore., and author of *The Cat Whisperer*. "It saves marriages."

Uncover Your Cat's Litter Box Preferences

To coax your cat back to his litter box, pick a cat litter the cat enjoys digging in. How do you determine Fluffy's litter and box preferences? Ask him. Without opposable thumbs, he can't answer an online survey. Simply open a cat litter smorgasbord.

• Set up a cafeteria-style line of three (or more) boxes side-by-side containing different styles of litter
  • Wait and watch

• Scoop once or twice a day. It's not hard to tell which are preferred and which litters are avoided like, well, lemon cat litter.

Tails from the Trenches

Dr. Susan Konecny, medical director of Best Friends Animal Society, said one client had a cat who began peeing and pooping outside the box for no apparent reason. "We suggested offering a 'litterbox cafeteria,' which included a variety of different litters in multiple pans in multiple locations. Once the cat consistently used the preferred litter, all boxes were switched to this nonscented litter. This solved the problem." Dr. Konecny learned after the fact that the client had initially been using heavily scented litter.

Use the same process to pick out a litter box. (Helpful Hint: If you buy a litter or box style your cat doesn't like, you can return it to most pet supply or discount stores within 30 days for a refund or credit. Keep your receipt.)

If Fluffy isn't impressed by commercially available litters (including Dr. Elsey's), try filling the litter box with some nontraditional textures, such as puppy pads, cloth baby diapers, dirty clothes or towels, newspapers, cardboard, soiled carpet, potting soil, sand, or even an empty litter box. Fill the box with whatever texture he's been going on. (Check out how to move from dirty clothes to a litter box in Chapter 15 Litter Box Rehab.)

Switching Litter Brands

If you want to switch your cat's litter, veterinary researcher Tony Buffington suggests placing the new litter in a different container next to the current box containing the old litter. This enables Fluffy to show you which litter he prefers. "Once you find a litter that your cat likes, don't change it (except as a choice) or the cat might refuse to use the litter box," he said.

Litter Accessories Your Cat Despises

Even things not directly associated with the litter box can cause your cat to seek comfort in another location.

• Litter box liners: Avoid litter box liners. Cats hate the urine splashback, as well as getting their nails stuck in the plastic.

• Litter mats: They can also make your kitty rebel. Like coarse cat litters, some mat textures can feel unbearable. "Some mats are sharp and spiky," Adelman said. "It's like having to walk over hot coals to go to the bathroom. You're not going to do that; you're going to pee in the sink. So is your cat. The mat is for you, so it should be comfortable for the cat."

Dr. Rigoni, owner of All Cats Veterinary Hospital in Houston, recommends using spongy (non-adhesive) shelf liners. They're so soft, the kitties don't mind stepping on them and the texture captures the litter.

In some households cats have a tendency to prefer to pee just outside of the box on the litter mat. For these pee-ers, I like the ❀Drymate® Cat Litter Mat (RPM, Inc. Drymate.com; 800-872-8201). Its soft felt-like, catches the litter, and the waterproof base protects the floor from box-side accidents. It's also machine washable.

• Scented additives: These are no substitutes for keeping the box clean. In addition, air fresheners should be set well away from the box in case cats do not like their smell.

Location, Location, Location

An inviting litter box involves more than size, style and smell. It's also about "where." The cat's bathrooms should be easily accessible, set up in areas where Fluffy feels safe. When people place litter boxes out of sight because they don't want to see or smell them, they may unintentionally cause a crisis for the cat.

Provide one litter box for each cat, plus one extra. But if you have three cats, you can't simply place four boxes in a cluster. While they may be easier to clean if they're clustered together, it's better for your kitty (and your carpet) if you set them up in multiple locations throughout the house. This prevents a dog or dominant cat from guarding all the boxes at once.

Keep in mind, low-traffic doesn't mean so remote the cat needs camping gear to trek there. Kitties shouldn't have to climb Mt. Everest or descend into the Marianas Trench to answer the call of nature—especially seniors and kittens. To add insult to expedition, some cats must go through a cat flap to reach the toilet in the garage. That may work for some cats, but other kitties are afraid of them.

Dr. Siracusa said it's not OK to have the cat's core area (with his bed and toys) in the living room, but the box in the basement. "We have to increase the motivation to use the litter box."

Translation: Place a box on every floor of the house.

Tails from the Trenches

One cat behaviorist had a client whose older cat was peeing at the base of the stairs. The man had two litter boxes, one upstairs and another in the back of the house. The behaviorist instructed him to thoroughly clean the soiled areas and to add a third litter box at the bottom of the stairs. The third more-accessible litter box resolved the issue.

Another huge turn-off is when people put the food bowls immediately next to the box. You don't want to eat in the bathroom; neither does your cat. Place food and water bowls at least three feet away from the litter box. Better still, move them to the opposite wall or a different room entirely.

Tails from the Trenches

Dr. Judy Morgan has four cats and four litter boxes, located in the basement to prevent the dogs from snacking from the box. She also feeds the cats in the basement. The cats' litter box accuracy was hit-and-miss. The cats started peeing in another area, far away from the food bowls. She moved the litter boxes to the area where they'd been peeing on the floor. The cats started batting 1000. "I just had to listen to what they were telling me about where the box needed to be placed," she said.

Feeling of Safety

A kitty may decide he doesn't like a location due to scary or painful experiences in the past, such as injuries caused by doors, a kid or another cat tormenting him, or even a painful bout of cystitis.

Safety, or lack thereof, is a state of mind to an inside kitty. As you know, free-roaming cats are prey, and are especially vulnerable when they squat to pee or poop. Just because you know there are no coyotes hovering near the litter box doesn't mean Fluffy won't worry about them. A quiet, open location will make your cat feel safer than a noisy or high-traffic area.

Avoid enclosed locales like closets, cabinets or small bathrooms where the cat could become trapped by kids or other pets. Placing the box in the back of an open room allows good visibility so kitty can see who's coming into the room. He'll feel safer if people and other animals can't sneak up on him mid-squat. This also offers multiple escape routes.

Keep litter boxes away from all appliances and air ducts that could startle Fluffy when they suddenly turn on. The laundry room works well for you because you don't have to deal with the odor, but an athletic shoe banging around in the clothes dryer or the washer working a spin cycle can scare the fur off a kitty.

Another surprising feline fear is pitch darkness. "While cats have great night vision, they can't see in total darkness," said Mieshelle Nagelschneider, author of *The Cat Whisperer and* behaviorist at The Cat Behavior Clinic in Portland. "They want to see where they're stepping to make sure there are no dinosaurs waiting for them."

Stormy, a black green-eyed kitty started pooping in front of his litter box, which had been set up deep inside a laundry room utility closet. "As soon as we put up a nightlight he started going inside and using the box," she said. "If there's no light available, move the box closer to the ambient light or get a cheap battery-powered light."

"When I'm not finding cat pee with my black light, I use it to brighten psychedelic posters from the 70's."

7   CRIME SCENE CLEANUP

Does the father figure in your cat's life ever clean the litter box? My husband claims that men lack the scooping gene.
~ Barbara L. Diamond

As happens at a violent crime scene, your home has become contaminated with bodily fluids (and solids). Until you *thoroughly* clean all soiled surfaces, both you and Fluffy will be condemned to constantly relive that vicious cycle of contamination and recontamination. Not to mention that constantly inhaling ammonia fumes is hazardous to both your lungs and Fluffy's.

As soon as you notice the mess, clean it up. Removing all traces of ammonia and pheromones from the carpet is the first step in persuading Fluffy to return to the litter box. After all, if it smells like a toilet, Fluffy will use it as a toilet."

Cat pee and poop in a carpet is like a ghost. It contains pheromones that continue to attract kitties to the soiled areas. It's as if the cat has posted an olfactory sign saying "Bathroom."

If you simply mask the pee odors, you may be able to fool your nose, but Fluffy, with his far superior sense of smell, will be able to find his alternate potty every time. In the words of veterinary behaviorist, Dr. Dodman, "He'll be drawn back to the spot like a heat-seeking missile to a source of heat."

Completely banishing the odor ghost requires treating the entire affected area, including the carpet pad and subflooring.

Crime Scene Cleanup Supplies

Your cleanup kit should include:
- Ultraviolet light
- Flashlight
- Masking tape
- Odor neutralizer
- Old sponges
- *White* towels or paper towels
- Spatula or putty knife
- Cheap, large crystal silica gel cat litter
- Mop

Before you can clean up the cat pee, you've got to find the pee spots—all of them. That's not as easy as it sounds. Hydrogen sulfide, a gas emitted by poop and pee, deadens the nerve endings in your nose. You may be able to smell ammonia, but your nose, confused by locations, can't pinpoint them. Fortunately, those inconspicuous pee spots are visible under the right conditions.

Under the Rug

The soiled area in the carpet resembles an iceberg; you are only seeing the tip. If the surface stain appears to be the size of a silver dollar, it has likely spread to dinner plate diameter beneath the pad. You must clean all layers. Even the best odor eliminator won't work if it doesn't fully saturate the soiled layers. You may want to use a large medical or cooking syringe (a needle is not necessary) to inject sufficient quantities of chemicals deep into the carpet pad.

When the ammonia odor persists or your cat returns to a spot, pull the carpet up and treat the wood or concrete subflooring. When the subfloor has dried, seal it, then saturate the carpet with odor removers. Failing that, you may need to replace floor boards, in addition to carpeting and padding. Don't forget to scrub the walls and baseboards. You may have to treat the carpet multiple times in order to pass feline muster.

You can safely and cheaply remove cat pee from your concrete slab by steeping it with hydrogen peroxide. It will "boil" on contact. Repeat the process until you can apply the peroxide without a boiling reaction. My industry specialist said it may take a week of repeated treatments to thoroughly purge the odor. Once the odor has been removed from the foundation, apply a concrete sealer. This creates a vapor barrier.

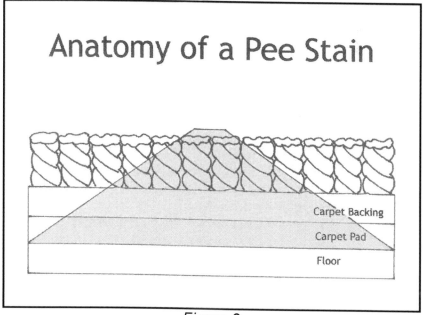

Figure 3

Cleaning a Recent Accident

When cleaning up a fresh mistake (translation: still wet), place a *white* cloth or paper towel over the spot and blot it by pressing down. Do this until you pull no more moisture from the carpet. ⚠Avoid printed designs or borders because the dye could bleed into a light-colored carpet. Also, don't rub the carpet with the cloth, as this will only force the pee farther from the original spot and deeper into the pad.

Stain removers—not always

"Stain removers" may take the visible stain out of an old mishap, but they can't replace the color once it's been bleached from the carpet fibers. Left untreated, cat pee will eventually fade the color—another reason to clean a pee spot as soon as you find it.

Killer Cleanup

You don't want your olfactory crime scene to become an accidental homicide, with Fluffy playing the part of the chalk outline. It's up to you to choose products that will not harm your cat and then follow the label instructions.

It can be tricky to use the label to determine if a product could harm your cat. Kitties are often more sensitive to chemicals than other animals, and understanding product labels almost requires a degree in chemistry!

Many chemicals are metabolized by the liver before being eliminated by the body, said Dr. Lynn Rolland Hovda, director of veterinary services at the Pet Poison Helpline. "Cats, in particular, lack some of the enzyme systems needed to make this change." A product that's perfectly safe for a 10-pound baby or even a 10-pound dog can be deadly to a cat because of their sensitivity.

If you're worried about using a product around Fluffy, call the manufacturer and ask how to use it safely around cats. The label lists the company's phone number. Also find out if the product should be rinsed and dried before allowing your cat access to the area. Call your local poison control number or American Association of Poison Control Centers (800-222-1222). Tell them it's not an emergency.

Before you buy a product, find out how it works; read the label warnings. These cautions list a cleaner's wide range of potential injuries, from irritation of the gastrointestinal tract to chemical burns in mouth, esophagus, and stomach. While the warnings are alarming, the more frightening part is they are intended for people. Your kitty is more at risk.

Labeling laws have been set up to protect humans, not pets. Some toxic but secret ingredients may not appear on the label. Watch for cautionary words such as "warning," or "danger" that indicate toxic contents. The word "caution" is of slightly less concern. It appears on products that can cause human gastric upset or eye irritation. "Flammable" or "combustible" products may contain dangerous solvents. Products with label statements regarding air quality danger or skin irritation or use in a well-ventilated room can cause respiratory irritation.

Next look at the ingredient list. You may not know what all the chemical names mean, but, look for ingredients ending in "-ol" or "-ene," which typically indicates toxic solvents. "Chlor" usually includes chlorine. "Glycols" contain petroleum-based ether. "Phenols," can include coal tar derivatives. None of these things are good for your cat.

If the label warns you to wear gloves or eye protection, "dilute," or "keep out of reach of children," you need to be concerned about the effect it would have should the cat accidentally come in contact with it.

Never allow your cat into areas where you use or store cleaners. Clean up spills of concentrated chemicals immediately so Fluffy doesn't walk across it and later ingest it while licking his paws.

Chemicals can be absorbed systemically through your cat's paw pads, or even when he walks through an area filled with fumes. A cat will be doubly exposed by licking the chemical from his paws or coat when he grooms himself.

"Cats should be removed from the environment where chemicals are being used and not returned until the area is dry, vacuumed if need be, and well ventilated," Dr. Hovda, the poison expert, said.

When you think it's clean, rinse again. The same logic should be used whether you're cleaning carpets or mopping the floor.

If the product label only lists warnings about pets walking on the wet carpet, it's usually safe for them to walk on once it has dried. "But the key word here is 'dry' and not semi-dry or damp," Dr. Hovda said. "If the product is meant to be vacuumed after it is dry, a thorough vacuuming should occur. Airing the area prior to letting a cat back in is a good idea as well. Absorption through skin also occurs fairly frequently, especially the ears, as cats respond to oral pain by pushing their face along the ground and into other things! Cats are notorious for grooming themselves and then rubbing their eyes, so ocular exposure may be a problem."

Avoid cleaners containing ammonia. Because cat pee contains ammonia, cleaning a pee stain with ammonia is the basically inviting your cat to refresh the spot with his own ammonia.

Use according to directions

Most products are safe for use around cats *when you follow the directions.* [WARNING!] Your cat gets into trouble when the label said to dilute 1 tablespoon per gallon, and for whatever reason you use a cup instead. Stronger isn't necessarily better. A chemical that is safe at a 1:20 dilution may burn your cat's skin at a higher concentration. Always color test the carpet or upholstered furniture before using a product.

Three factors determine the dosage of what is toxic to cats:

• Concentration: Is the concentration of the chemical 2 percent or 98 percent?

• Quantity: Did Fluffy get one or two licks or 2 tablespoons?

• Size of the cat: Is he a 2-pound kitten or a 14-pounder? Twelve pounds make a big difference.

Naturally Safe

You may turn to "natural" cleaners to protect Fluffy, but just because the active ingredient comes from a natural source doesn't ensure its safety. Hemlock and tobacco are natural but deadly. Manufacturers are not required to disclose ingredients contained in their products unless they are *dangerous to people*. Products labeled "green" may contain dyes, fragrances and detergents that are unsafe for kitties.

Cationic detergents, contained in many "natural" cleaning products, are safe around people and aren't required to be listed in the ingredients. However, they use strong acids, such as hydrochloric acid, as the neutralizing agent. These acids can burn your cat's skin and mouth.

"The severity of the burns depends on the concentration of the cationic detergent solution," Dr. Hovda said. "Oral exposure to concentrations of less than 2 percent can cause irritation to the mouth such as oral ulcers, throat inflammation. A 7.5 percent solution can cause corrosive burns to the mouth, tongue and esophagus *in most animals*. But feline exposure will be even more severe, not only because of their unique physiology, but because they groom themselves far more than other species of animal."

Commercial products don't have a monopoly on hazards. Even natural homemade cleaners have safety issues.

If ingested, even vinegar and water solutions can cause injury, vomiting, diarrhea and pain. Vinegar is acidic. Depending on the concentration, it can also cause burns or irritation to the mouth and skin.

Citrus cleaners make impressive kitchen degreasers, but in concentrated form, citrus can also cause skin and mouth burns and irritation. Read about citrus masking agents below.

How Different Odor Neutralizers Work

There are almost as many brands of odor neutralizers as there are breeds of dogs and cats combined. Each product reacts with odor molecules in a different way, with varying degrees of effectiveness. They eliminate, change, coat, absorb or mask odors, often in combinations.

Below are many different classes of odor product, how they work, and the advantages, disadvantages and limitations of each.

• **Molecular odor eliminators:** This class of product bonds with the odor molecules, permanently converting an odor molecule into a non-odor molecule. They aren't affected by chemicals previously applied to the carpet. They work immediately and permanently, but they are rather expensive. Ozone generators fit into this category. In my experience ❀Zero Odor (Zeroodorpet.com; 800-526-2967) is my favorite odor neutralizer. I also like the ❀CritterZone Air Naturalizer (AirRestore USA. CritterzoneUSA.com; 612-235-4911), a plug-in or battery-powered device.

• **Oxygenators:** These products cause a chemical reaction that adds oxygen to the odor molecule, changing its composition. These products break down odors into carbon dioxide and water. The process is frequently used in wastewater treatment plants and in the purification of drinking water. You can buy ready-to-use liquids or powders. ❀ Fizzion (Fizzion & Kegel; FizzionClean.com; 863-513-0087) is my preferred oxygenation odor eliminator for carpets.

• **Disinfectants:** Antibacterial agents kill the bacteria — the source of the odor. If the bacteria are destroyed, so is the odor. This is often the method of choice of many professional hoarder cleanup companies. Most bactericides can be used on soiled spots with results in under an hour, some even quicker. The carpet should then be cleaned immediately and liquids extracted. The labels usually instruct you to remove pets from premises, ventilate closed spaces, and only allow pets on flooring after it is completely dry. Some of these chemicals are very toxic. [WARNING!] Allow the floor to *thoroughly* dry before giving pets access. Neither carpet cleaning products nor pesticides affect the effectiveness of most antibacterials. Start light, and use the weakest formulation. If that doesn't work, reapply with slightly stronger application. Disinfectants should not be used full-strength. Check the label. Use according to directions.

• **Enzymatics:** Enzymes are made of proteins that work like saliva, breaking down the odor molecules, but they do not digest it. Since they're not living organisms, they're not vulnerable to chemicals and extreme heat and cold, like live bacteria. Chemicals in other products, such as detergents and pesticides, won't affect the enzymes. Enzymes will dissolve detergent residue from earlier carpet cleanings.

Enzymes are pH sensitive, and pH fluctuates as the odor breaks down, working best at a neutral pH between 6 and 8. They only work when they are moist, and, like bacteria, can take about 24 hours to break down odor molecules. This could cause a mold problem in hot humid climates.

• **Bacteria-only:** These solutions contain bacteria that break down the odor and consume it. These strains of bacteria are not hazardous to your health. Manufacturers have strict regulatory standards under which they operate, and the nonpathogenic or "friendly" bacteria have been laboratory-tested for safety. When bacteria finish their job, they're gone. Unfortunately, bacteria are delicate life forms with short life spans and can die before the job is finished, so you may have to keep treating the spot. It takes about 24 hours for the bacteria to work, and they can only work while the carpet is moist. You may have to place a damp towel over the treated area to keep it from drying out too quickly. In certain environments you may run the risk of growing mold or mildew. These solutions often contain added fragrance, because the ammonia intensifies while the odor molecules are breaking down. Without the perfume, the smell could knock you over with a litter scoop.

Check the product label for "use by" dates. Storage is critical because some bacteria are light and heat sensitive. Bacterial products have a limited shelf life and are sensitive to temperature extremes. Store at room temperature. Chemicals or detergents previously used on the carpet will kill bacteria.

• **Bacterial/enzyme combinations:** Some products team bacteria and enzymes together to create a digestive food fest. Enzymes break down the molecules the way our saliva begins the digestive process, then bacteria consumes the organic material. The fluids turn into CO_2 and water, which then evaporates. With the food source eaten and the carpet dry, the bacteria die.

Unfortunately, the bacteria can die before the odor has been completely removed, so you must keep the carpet moist (not necessarily wet) and add fresh solution for at least 24 hours. Once again, you may have mildew problems if you live in a hot, humid climate.

A large older stain may require 32 ounces of the bacterial/enzyme solution to do the job. If, after 24 hours, you still smell pee, you didn't use enough product. I have found ❀Urine Erase® (Reidell Chemicals Limited. Reidell.com; 519-285-2083 in Canada) was the most effective bacteria/enzyme neutralizer with a peroxide component. ❀Urine-Off™ Odor & Stain Remover (Bio-Pro Research, LLC. Urine-Off.com; 877-874-6363) is a bio-enzymatic cleaner containing enzymes, bacteria and minty surfactants.

• **Encapsulators:** In the encapsulation process, a molecule attaches to and surrounds the odor molecule with a bubble, blocking the odor. It removes the odor immediately, but the effects are often temporary. The encapsulating molecule may eventually release its hold on the odor molecule, and the odor returns to its original shape and smell. Encapsulators may help out when the carpet smells and surprise company is on the way, but they're not a long-term solution. This type of product is not affected by the heat or cold, and has a shelf life of many years.

• **Deodorizer/Masking Agents:** These products use fragrance to cover up a stinky molecule with a pleasant-smelling molecule. The foul reality is temporarily overpowered by the fragrant smoke screen. As with encapsulators, the odor's true nature will eventually rear its ugly nose. When the masking perfume wears off, the odor of cat pee will return with its previous robust potency.

Deodorizers usually contain fragrances, alcohol and water, which mask the odor-causing molecules but do not change them. These products may fool *your* nose, but not your cat's. He knows where to find the pee.

Most people believe that citrus eliminates odors, but it's actually a masking agent. It basically gives you orange-scented poop. The strong scent simply blocks the olfactory senses and the person temporarily can't smell the cat pee. (That's why citrus acts as a cat repellent. In the wild a cat must be able to smell larger predators and his mousey meal. Citrus temporarily compromises that ability to smell. Not being able to smell prey or larger predators puts a natural cat in peril.) So think twice about using it in or around litter boxes. Although there's no guarantee, cleaning with citrus might discourage kitties from hanging out on counters and other off-limits areas.

• **Absorbents:** Absorbents remove odor with a positive-negative ion reaction—like a magnet that straps to the odor molecule. Enough chemistry mumbo jumbo. Baking soda and the volcanic ash Zeolite are two of the most popular absorption products. They usually come in powder or larger granules. Sprinkle the powders on the carpet, leave for an hour or so, and vacuum. This is probably helpful to freshen up. Because odor is picked up rather than removed, you will need to continue to treat.

• **Detergents:** Detergent cleaners and odor absorbers (such as foaming spray carpet cleaners) use surfactants to loosen organic material and dirt from fabrics, but some odor may remain. They may contain cationic detergents that can burn your cat's skin or mouth.

The Poop on Poo

Poop comes in two forms: firm and easy to clean, and runny and disgusting to clean. With a firm poop, pick it up with a paper towel or a plastic bag and spot clean the carpet with any cat-safe carpet spotter or cleaner, or even detergent. Unlike pee, this is a surface issue. [WARNING!] Always wash your hands after handling poop as it may contain organisms that could infect you.

Diarrhea in carpet is a whole different animal. Don't rub it in. Cover it with silica gel crystal litter to pull out the moisture. After a few minutes, run a putty knife or a spatula underneath the mess and lift it up. Saturate the area with your preferred odor neutralizer. Let it sit as directed by label. ⚠Blot (don't rub) with a *white* towel or paper towel. When you don't get any more moisture, saturate the area again. It's only clean when you aren't picking up colored liquid.

Wood and Laminate Flooring

Wood plank, parquet, and laminate flooring are popular in many multicat homes, but they're more temperamental to clean than carpeting. A couple of well-placed piddles can permanently damage your wood floor, visually as well as olfactorily.

When you find a puddle, wipe it up immediately. Follow with a clean moist paper towel. Then spray your favorite odor remover on the floor.

A wood floor with a longtime pet stain is a no-win scenario. Your flooring manufacturer probably says don't use water-based odor eliminators on their product. The manufacturers of odor eliminators echo the message. They tell you to clean with recommended cleaners. But the recommended cleaners don't contain anything that can neutralize the pee. They're both covering their tails legally. Effective odor products may damage your beautiful wood floor, but if you don't use them, your floor will retain that ammonia bouquet. Your wood floor has tiny cracks between the planks where liquid collects, inviting your kitties to come back and pee.

Before I surrendered and replaced my wood parquet floor with ceramic tile, I used ✿Simple Solution® Hardfloors Stain + Odor Remover (SimpleSolution.com; 800-448-8552) and ✿Zero Odor. ⚠This is off-label and you risk damaging your finish. Tough choice, but you have to make it.

At Your Service (Carpet Cleaning Companies)

If your carpet is too heavily soiled, you may need to bring in a professional carpet cleaning company to completely remove urine odor. Before hiring a company, find out what kind of chemicals the company plans to use. Ask your veterinarian or ASPCA/APCC to see if those chemicals are safe. Also, check with your local Better Business Bureau (BBB.org) for complaints.

8 CAT TAGGING: WHEN KITTY MARKS

I have just pissed into the Rhine River. For God's sake, send some gasoline.
~General George S. Patton, March 24, 1945

Cat pee happens. According to veterinary behaviorist Dr. Andrew Luescher, in 25 percent of single cat homes, the cat occasionally sprays.

"Urine marking is probably the most common form of inappropriate elimination," veterinary behaviorist Nicholas Dodman said. "Fortunately, research into feline behavior has shown us why they spray, which gives us a number of treatment options." Dr. Dodman said with appropriate treatment, almost all urine-marking cats can be successfully treated.

Everybody Marks Territory

Before you come down on Fluffy for spraying, remember this: Everyone marks territory—including you. The 4-year-old scribbles on the walls with crayons, teenager spray paints buildings and fences. When adults move into new homes, we landscape, install new flooring and hang family photos. Even wedding rings display a form of territorial marking. Without an opposable thumb to work the aerosol can, kitties have to find another way to mark. That leaves bodily fluids.

Patton Pending

Figure 4 - Gen. George S. Patton pees in the Rhine River to notify Hitler he's taking German territory. Army censors airbrushed the pee stream from the photo. Because this is a book about the call of nature, I reinserted the pee using the stream from a lower resolution photograph.
Photo courtesy of the Weekly Standard.

My favorite examples of human marking parallel feline spraying in every way. During World War II, Gen. George S. Patton ordered the construction of a pontoon bridge to connect the banks of the Rhine River at Nierstein. As Patton's jeep reached the bridge's midpoint, he ordered his driver to stop. There, for the benefit of cameras, Ol' Blood 'n Guts pissed in the Rhine.

After the crossing, Patton sent this message to Gen. Dwight D. Eisenhower: "Dear SHAEF (Supreme Headquarters Allied Expeditionary Force), I have just pissed into the Rhine River. For God's sake, send some gasoline." The photo above is the edited version (Patton's urine stream was originally eliminated by an Army censor). There's no question he intended for Hitler to see his biological condemnation.

Patton's wasn't the only urine deposited on Nazi territory. British Prime Minister Winston Churchill actually beat Patton to the piss. Three weeks earlier, Churchill inspected the front lines near Jülich. There, sans cameras, Churchill not only whizzed on the anti-tank dragon's teeth lining Hitler's Siegfried Line, he also invited Field Marshalls Monty Montgomery and Alan Brooke to join him. Brooke, chief of the Imperial General Staff, said in his book *War Diaries, 1939-1945: Field Marshall Lord Alanbrooke*, "I shall never forget the childish grin of intense satisfaction that spread all over his face as he looked down at the critical moment."

Too much information? Maybe, but I want you to understand that people mark territory, and sometimes in exactly the same way kitties do.

Bite Me

Cats, even amorous or territorial cats, don't want to get into a fang-and-claw battle. Before cats fight, they posture: stalking, growling, yowling and trying to intimidate each other with an uncomfortable stare. If neither cat backs down, then the brawl begins. The attacker leaps for his opponent's neck. The defensive cat assumes a tummy-up position. No belly rubs for this guy; he's bringing all of his weapons to bear on his adversary. The aggressor has to get past those slice-'em-dice-'em claws and needle-sharp teeth. The aggressor will take "bite my butt" seriously and receive bites to his rear, while the defensive cat will likely suffer neck bites.

Domestic cats seldom fight to the death. Generally, the battle lasts only seconds. However, infection and broken teeth make both the champion and the loser more vulnerable to predators and other cats. It's better to intimidate your adversary from a distance with the impressive essence of your pee.

Complex Cat Pee

Unlike humans, who mark to make a visual statement, kitties communicate with one another remotely using pheromones produced by glands located on their face, paws and at the base of the tail. These glands produce data-rich scents that are unique to each cat, like an olfactory fingerprint.

All pheromones are not created equal. Pheromones generated near the corner of the mouth or from the side of the forehead near the temples are good-natured, calming pheromones that say, "You're my friend" or "You belong to me." (I discuss calming synthetic facial pheromones later in this chapter in Pheromones.) The paw pads secrete "alarm pheromones" warning other cats to avoid danger. We're most interested in the messages sent in cat pee that snarl, "Piss off" or "Let's make kittens!"

Spraying is an efficient, no-nonsense form of communication in feline hierarchies and territories. An outside cat hoses down trees, tires, rocks, fences and objects that have already been sprayed by other cats. He sprays the perimeter of his territory to warn other cats to stay out. He might issue a pee-scented challenge when he's considering taking over another cat's turf. (Think Patton). It's also thought when a cat feels anxious, spraying comforts him by surrounding himself with a familiar scent. Spraying may be normal behavior outside, but inside your home such bold statements aren't appreciated.

You and I are olfactorily challenged. Based on the way a cat's olfactory system is structured and the amount of brain power interpreting smell, it's reasonable to assume that a cat's sense of smell is more like a dog's than a human's. Humans possess an unimpressive 5 million odor-sensitive cells in our noses, compared with a cat's 200 million.

Dr. Karen L. Overall, a board certified applied animal behaviorist on the faculty of the Center for Neurobiology and Behavior in the Psychiatry Department at Penn Med, said, "Urine contains all the metabolic byproducts of anything that goes through the blood. It contains hormones, including things like cortisol, a hormone indicative of a stress state and a particular molecular process. So cats can learn a lot about the internal state of other cats and what is going on in their heads by sniffing urine. Feces contain the breakdown products of eating. So . . . you can find out what was eaten when, and may be able to track it back to its source. Also, you can tell if an animal is ill or well based on digestion. Finally, because neurochemical patterns can be signatures, urine IDs an individual whose internal state, health and food you can now follow."

When Fluffy deposits his scent, he reveals very specific facts to a potential mate or competitor without risking a violent encounter, the feline version of Facebook. They can threaten each other and talk smack without the danger of face-to-face combat.

Wild cats use their sense of smell in the same way people keep up with what's happening in the world via the Internet. Kitties sniff the latest news, traffic reports (which cats have traveled through his territory), grocery ads (a mouse left droppings here a few hours ago), war report (that tom from down the street has crossed the line and wants to kick tail), and even KittyMingle.com. (Woohoo, Misty's in heat again!)

Snipping It in the Bud

The first step to gaining control of your home is to get everyone fixed. Unaltered cats are going to spray. Period. A horny male will whiz "looking for love" messages as long as he has all his reproductive equipment. Eligible females will spray, "In heat. Looking for a hookup." However, in a study led by B.L. Hart, director of the Center for Animal Behavior at the UC Davis College of Biological Sciences, 90 percent of spraying males significantly reduced or completely stopped urine marking after a surgical attitude adjustment. In his article "Feline Behavior Problems," Dr. Luescher said 95 percent of females either ceased to spray or greatly reduced their spraying after being spayed.

Tails from the Trenches

Lacy's family was done with her. The Siamese-mix took "love your neighbor" to the extreme, leaving urinary calling cards all over the house hoping to attract boyfriends. The family didn't believe in spaying pets, but they expected Lacy to act as if she had been. They told me, if I didn't take her they were going to euthanize her. First stop was the animal hospital for corrective surgery. Despite being 5 years old, Lacy never soiled the house again. A short time later she went to a more deserving home.

In another case, 2-year-old intact Red also came home with me and immediately marked my favorite chair. Once again, an appointment was made and Red said good-bye to "the boys." Problem solved. I don't know if he was afraid I was going to cut off something else or simply no longer felt the need, but he turned into a perfect gentleman.

Altering your cat won't instantly stop marking urges. It can take a month or longer for the hormones to dissipate. Mature males like Red, whose veins flow heavy with testosterone, will take longer to clear out than a pubescent 5-month-old. Adjust your expectations accordingly. It's estimated that 10 percent of neutered males and 5 percent of spayed females still spray as a form of communication.

Although rare, occasionally a vet may miss testicular tissue during neuter surgery, and a male may continue to act, smell and spray like an intact boy. If you suspect your cat is still pumping testosterone, ask your vet to order a testosterone test. Also, most testosterone-producing males will have barbs on the penis. Have your vet cop a feel.

Why Do Housecats Spray?

Neutering and spaying can significantly decrease spraying, but it doesn't always stop this normal communication behavior. In an altered cat, spraying may indicate illness or some hard-to-handle stresses. (Please read Chapter 9: Hurry Up in There! Potty Issues in the Multipet Home, and all three of the medical chapters, So Sick It's Criminal and Senior Moments.)

I know *you* know what stress is because you deal with crazy relatives, tyrannical bosses and unreasonable customer service reps. But with a 16-hour sleep schedule, when does Fluffy have time to squeeze in a bout of anxiety? During the other eight hours.

Because cats are prey, Fluffy spends his entire life worrying about falling victim to larger carnivores. We know there are no cat-hunting predators in our homes, so the things that make them feel vulnerable might surprise us. A big one is change. Cats are creatures of habit. They respond with apprehension to changes we humans might not even notice, such as moving a chair across the room or putting a clean quilt on the bed. From Fluffy's perspective, major changes, such as a new spouse, pet, baby, remodeling or even outside activities may foreshadow the end of the world as he knows it.

When your cat feels distressed or harassed, he may seek out his favorite person's dirty clothes or linens and spray them because he finds comfort in the two blended smells. Or he may go the opposite route and scent-mark stuff that smells like the person or animal he's afraid of. When new objects appear in the home, Fluffy may need to anoint them, or he might hose the couch after guests have left to make the cushions smell "right" again.

A little old-fashioned detective work can provide leads to the source of Fluffy's stress. Use a crime scene staple, the black light, in a darkened room to scan for feline DNA. If the spray spots are primarily on the perimeter walls, especially near doors and windows, Fluffy is likely responding to an outdoor intruder encroaching on his turf. Marking the interior walls or prominent objects in the home's core points to intercat aggression or anxiety about people, pets or changes in the home.

With this is in mind, retrieve your questions and answers from Chapter 2: Gathering Evidence & Looking for Motive. It will help you backtrack and uncover what's ruffling Fluffy's whiskers. If you catch him mid-spray, try to recall what happened 30 minutes before his aerosol expression.

Things or changes that could cause stress marking include:
• Conflict or territorial disputes between cats (staring, hissing, spitting, growling, swatting)
   • A cat or other pet blocking access to the litter box or food and water
   • Separation anxiety
   • Change in feeding, litter box cleaning routines or regular playtime with you
   • Change in your work shifts
   • Dirty litter box
   • New baby, pet, human significant other
   • Death or illness of a pet or human family member
   • Kid left for college
   • Visits from neighborhood cats or wildlife
   • Move to a new home
   • Changes around the house, home remodeling, new furniture or carpet
   • You threw out that ugly chair Fluffy liked to scratch
   • Had houseguests or threw a party
   • Travel
   • Conflict among human family members
   • Switching from the summer bedspread to a winter quilt

This is just a cursory list, intended to make you think. Your kitty could be bothered by something more obvious or much more subtle. Remember to rule out medical problems that may also lead to urine marking. (See Chapters 10, 11 and 12 about medical issues).

Common Sense Hygiene

One study led by P.A. Pryor, an assistant professor in the Department of Veterinary Clinical Services at Washington State University, investigated how environmental management affects urine marking. The most common causes of spraying in the study cats "were agonistic interactions with other cats outside or inside the home." When owners "scooped waste from the litter box daily, and changed the litter and cleaned the litter box weekly," the frequency of urine marking was significantly reduced—by environmental management alone. So treatment should include basic hygiene.

Outside access

If you have a securely fenced yard you can install an ❧Affordable Cat Fence (CatFence.com; 210-736-2287 or 888-840-2287,) which should keep your cat inside the yard and keep other cats out. (Read about these devices in Chapter 13 Environmental Enrichment: Just What the Doctor Ordered. Cats allowed outside are less likely to spray.

Multicat Stress

Just as people become stressed and irritable when we're crammed into airplanes like peanuts in a can, cats—being territorial creatures—become stressed when living in an overcrowded home. There's a strong correlation between the number of cats in the home and spraying. In fact, the frequency of spraying escalates as the number of cats in the home increases.

Both housecats and outside kitties have overlapping territories and they "time share" real estate. Regardless of where they live, cats are creatures of routine, and in the wild they depend on a schedule to avoid direct conflict with another cat. Marking territory allows them to post information without having to come face-to-face, like roommates hanging a tie on the door to avoid interruption.

Cats spray inside the home for the same reason they spray outside—to mark ownership, post a warning, or even signal a turf-takeover. Don't be surprised if your sprayer(s) feels protective about who approaches his valuable assets. The other cats will spray in response.

Cats also spray to show dominance, like enemy gangs tagging buildings in a rival neighborhood. Basically that's what happens when you have many cats jockeying for position and fighting over resources. The keys to turning off the spray paint spigots lie in reducing stress and creating an abundance of resources.

Experts agree that cats need privacy, abundant territory and a safe place to go to the bathroom. "All kitties need food, a safe resting place, scratching post, and social interaction with the owner," said Niwako Ogata, BVSc, PhD, DACVB. Dr. Ogata is an assistant professor in companion animal behavior at the Purdue University College of Veterinary Medicine. "Cats shouldn't have to compete over resources. Most cats want to have access to a window. Provide cat grass and resting places in three dimensions."

An environment of plenty provides lower-ranked cats with hiding areas, food, water and litter boxes. Place these resources in multiple rooms so shy cats aren't forced to cross paths with more dominant cats just to eat or go to the bathroom. Provide one litter box per cat plus one extra in a different place (not clustered together). (Read more about abundant resources in Chapter 13 Environmental Enrichment: Just What the Doctor Ordered and Chapter 9 Hurry Up in There! Potty Issues in the Multipet Home.)

Pheromones

Earlier I mentioned that kitties have scent glands on their face that contain friendly pheromones. Whenever your cat weaves around your legs or head bumps you, he's telling the world you belong to him. Not just a possession; you're his friend. These peaceable pheromones make him feel calm and safe and in the company of friends.

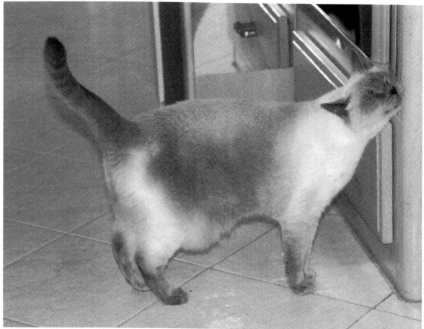

Figure 5 - Sam deposits facial pheromones on the corner of the kitchen cabinet. Photo by Weems S. Hutto.

After cleaning pee and spray stains (Learn how to remove pheromones from the carpet in Chapter 7 Crime Scene Cleanup), you may help reduce stress by spraying some pheromones yourself.

✿Comfort Zone® with Feliway® (Central Garden & Pet Company www.petcomfortzone.com 800-234-2269) is a synthetic copy of a cat's friendly facial pheromones. This analogue fools a kitty into thinking that *he* has deposited the scent. Not only do these pheromones promote calm, but kitties seldom spray or eliminate in a spot that's already been marked with facial pheromones.

Many of the country's leading experts on inappropriate elimination and feline behavior, including Drs. Neilson, Hunthausen and Ogata, recommend using Feliway® to reduce stress and urine marking. And unlike antianxiety drugs, there are no apparent negative side effects.

Feliway comes in a pump spray (nice little irony). Spritz it on previously marked spots and/or prominent locations at about nose height to a kitty every day until you start to notice head bumping or authentic facial marking, or use the Feliway diffuser like a plug-in air freshener near the targeted zone. The diffuser, while more expensive, requires less effort. It fills a 700-square-foot room with the friendly pheromones. Because cats don't want to toilet where facial pheromones have been deposited, never use Feliway near litter boxes.

The studies of Feliway have had mixed results. Some of the better results show an 80 to 90 percent success rate. Others have shown no success at all. A 2000 study conducted by Wayne Hunthausen, DVM, showed that out of 50 households, 33 percent of the cats in the Feliway study stopped spraying. In other studies held in the U.S., United Kingdom, France and Japan, cat owners saw between 74 percent to 97 percent reduction in spraying. Even a reduction in spraying will improve everyone's quality of life.

Because habits aren't formed overnight, they also take time to break. You may be able to stop using Feliway about three months after the cats have calmed down. In some situations it's not practical to use sprays and plug-ins. In those cases, or if kitties don't respond to Feliway, I recommend the ❀SENTRY® Calming collar (SentryPetCare.com; 800-224-7387), which uses a different synthetic feline pheromone. I have an aggressive blind kitty named BK who seldom antagonizes the other cats when wearing a fresh Calming Collar. My success aside, this product does not have the research studies to back it up.

These pheromone diffusers and collars don't work magically. Without implementing a program of environmental enrichment that includes an abundance of resources and better litter boxes, pheromones are useless. They are more likely to be effective as part of a *program* of improvements.

Can't We Just Get Along?

In multiple pet homes, you may experience dominance aggression or territorial aggression. Territorial aggression most often occurs in a home with more than one intact male, when a new cat joins the family or a cat smells different after a trip to the vet. The outdated concept, "Let them work it out" doesn't solve the problem any better than letting a school bully or a cyber bully work it out with their victims. Victims only win in the movies. Why not try reconciliation? More serious social conflicts may require you to completely separate the feuding cats and reintroduce them gradually. (I talk about how to do this in Chapter 9 Hurry Up in There! Potty Issues in the Multipet Home.)

Dr. Ogata said the ideal treatment not only provides an acceptable territory, but also addresses the aggression and anxiety. That may require pharmacological treatment. She warns that drug treatment doesn't work on its own. You need to address the root causes of the cat's fear and anxiety.

Outside Intruders

One situation that will make any feline go ballistic is the presence of a stray cat or dog, or wildlife taunting him through the window. No self-respecting cat is going to sit quietly by and let a feline General Patton pee in *his* yard. Because your cat is trapped inside your home, his only option is to spray the inside locations where he smells the invader (windows, windowsills, blinds, drapes and doors). Your 10-pound cat is willing to confront an invader of much greater strength to defend his territory. If that can't happen, he'll take it out on kitty companions or spray the curtains.

Figure 6 - Mugsy challenges an 8-foot alligator. Photo courtesy of Lori Blair and Cajun Pride Swamp Tours in Laplace, La.

Around 2008, someone abandoned a 2-year-old gray tabby at Cajun Pride Swamp Tours near LaPlace, Louisiana. The tour grounds is a popular dumping location for unwanted cats, so tour owner Chris Smits welcomed the newcomer to his clowder of strays. Smits named the new cat Mugsy because "he was running the park like a little gangsta."

It quickly became apparent that Mugsy was territorial on a colossal scale. This feline Chuck Norris showed alligator wrangling abilities that would have made the late Steve Irwin envious. When the alligators eased out of the water into Mugsy's territory, the cat ambushed them, hissing and swatting the gators on the nose or head, forcing them back into the swamp.

The first time Mugsy charged a gator, Smits was certain it wouldn't end well for the tabby, but Mugsy stood his ground and the giant reptile retreated. "I thought he was a little bit crazy," Smits said

After two years of sending alligators running, Mugsy appeared in a YouTube video www.youtube.com/watch?v=5sAF8gMN9c0 that has received over 11 million views. Smits said when a gator came out of the water near a young boy, Mugsy jumped into action to protect him. The video didn't capture that, but it did show Mugsy swatting a 5-foot alligator and the alligator retreating beneath the water's surface. A few seconds later, the gator returned with a friend and Mugsy confronted both of them, sending them off with their tails figuratively between their legs.

FYI, when Smits sold the tour business, Mugsy retired from gator wrestling and went to live with his family.

Mugsy isn't alone. Although your Fluffy may not challenge 10-foot-iong reptiles with a bite force more than 2,000 pounds per square inch, he probably feels as protective of his own yard as Mugsy did about his boat ramp.

If alligators or other fauna bring out your cat's inner fire hose, here are some things you can try.

Repel intruders

Set up deterrents to prevent animals from coming into your yard. Place battery-operated deterrents like the ❧ScareCrow® Motion-Activated Animal Deterrent (Contech Electronics Inc. ConTech-inc.com; 800-767-8658) ❧CatStop™ Ultrasonic Cat Deterrent (ConTech-inc.com) in the yard to deter visiting cats. CatStop is a loud ultrasonic motion-activated cat repellent that emits a frequency too high for humans to hear. (Read about animal repellents in Chapter 15 Litter Box Rehab.)

Limit Fluffy's view

Start by barring Fluffy's view of the intruders. On the ground floor, try blocking the bottom half of the window with the opaque window film (Decorativefilm.com.) You could also use foil, shutters, blinds or curtains.

Make windowsills inaccessible by blocking them with chairs or other furniture. While these can limit Fluffy's visual access, he may still be able to smell his tormentor.

You may not need to block his outside view entirely. Fluffy may be less stressed if he views the yard from above, such as a tall cat condo or second-story window. This places Fluffy in a position of comfort and control, rather than at eye level. If that doesn't work, block all access to windows where the intruders appear, or keep him out of that room. The stray may show up at the same time every day, so make the room off limits at times the intruder is most likely to prowl. After sunset, use your black light to locate spray spots outside the house left by animal intruders. Be especially careful to clean the stains near windows and doors where your kitty can smell it. Next, use the techniques I discuss in Chapter 14: Outside Cats and Restraining Orders to repel four-legged trespassers.

Restrict Fluffy's access to the target room. Lock the offending cat out of the room when you can't be there to watch him, or confine him to a single room to limit the territory he needs to defend. Cats urine mark areas as they patrol their territory. It's a remote warning because they can't always be there to banish an intruder. If he's confined to a single room, Fluffy can always be present to defend it. He won't need to post any yellow "No Trespassing" signs.

If you can't keep him out of the room, make just the target spots unpleasant with:

🐾 Sticky Paws® XL (Pioneer Pet; Pioneerpet.com; 866-317-6278)

🐾 Ssscat, a motion-activated pressurized air repellent, in the area he sprays

- Plastic carpet protectors with the pointy side up
- Aluminum foil
- Adhesive shelf paper, sticky side up
- Bubble wrap
- Solid orange air freshener
- Strong cologne on a cotton ball

Changing the Room's Context

Changing your cat's perception of the room he's been marking may reduce his need to spray. Cats seldom spray where they eat, sleep or scratch. Please be patient. No approach works on every cat every time. Some of these strategies may solve your problems; other kitties respond by backing up to the wall and turning on the hoses. Only your cat will know for sure. Here are some things to try:

- Over the area where he would stand to spray his favorite target, encourage a friendlier form of marking such as facial rubbing and scratching. Try spritzing the synthetic facial pheromone ❀Comfort Zone with Feliway ❀SENTRY® Good Behavior Pheromone Sprays for Cats or diffuser (SentryPetCare.com; 800-224-7387) in areas that have been pee-marked and prominent locations every day until you notice Fluffy personally face marking in the area. (If you can't refresh the area daily, try plug-in diffusers.)

• Self grooming brushes like ❀The Purrfect Arch (As Seen on TV. AsSeenOnTV.com) and ❀Catit Self Groomer (Rolf C. Hagen CatIt.com; 800-724-2436) also inspire face marking.

• Promote paw marking by placing sturdy scratching posts or more economical options like cardboard scratching pads in the area. (The Test Kitties like the ❀Ultimate Scratching Post (Pioneer Pet PioneerPet.com; 866-317-6278) and ❀M.A.X. scratchers from Cat Claws (CatClaws.com; 800-783-0977) because they have both horizontal and vertical scratching surfaces and a hidey hole.

• Set up an easy-to-clean legal spraying station, basically a kitty bulletin board. Encourage marking in this specific spot with whatever substance Fluffy likes to mark (plastic grocery bags, newspapers, dirty clothes, etc.).

• After cleaning the floor, place food (or a food puzzle) and water bowls directly over Fluffy's preferred spraying place. You could also feed him by dropping dry food directly on the floor. There's an additional list of strategies for stopping the marking in Chapter 6 Thinking Inside the Litter Box.

• Hold a catnip party. (I explain that in Chapter 13 Environmental Enrichment: Just What the Doctor Ordered.

• Get his blood pumping. Most of us feel great after a good workout to get your heart pumping. So do kitties. Exercise releases serotonin and many other chemicals, which promotes a feeling of well-being in humans and kitties. Naturally, Fluffy's not going to lift weights or do calisthenics. But you can get his blood flowing, relieve stress, dampen aggression and squelch spraying, all with the flick of a cat toy. Feather toys, toys on a string or wand are perfect to make kitties run, jump, and leap—thus using up calories and wearing themselves out—and are ideal solutions to pent-up stress. Twenty minutes of active play with a toy like ❀Da Bird (10 minutes, twice a day) will help vent some of that energy that the bully would have spent harassing the subordinate cats.

Figure 7 - Riou feels no pain during a therapeutic catnip session. Photo by Weems S. Hutto.

As an added bonus, encourage play inside the area that the cat(s) like to hose. Do whatever you can to turn the soiled area into part of the cat's main territory. (I talk about games you can play with your kitties in Chapter 13 Environmental Enrichment: Just What the Doctor Ordered.)

• **Place a deep plastic box in the immediate area where the cat is spraying.** Premark the box with Fluffy's scent by putting a little of his pee in it. The high sides let him stand and spray the walls inside the litter box.

(If you need more detailed information about living in a multicat family, I devoted the next chapter and my entire book *Cat Wrangling Made Easy: Maintaining Peace and Sanity in Your Multicat Home* to the topic.)

"Hey! Hurry up in there! There's a line!"

9 HURRY UP IN THERE! POTTY ISSUES IN THE MULTIPET HOME

Most beds sleep up to six cats. Ten cats without the owner.
~ Stephen Baker

Inappropriate elimination in a multicat home takes on all the twists and turns of a world class suspense novel. It may require the skills of Sherlock Holmes to determine who's the victim, who's the innocent bystander, and which one of your little darlings is the perpetrator. After all, your witnesses aren't talking.

If you grew up with siblings, you likely know about competition for the bathroom. Older sis takes an hour and a half to fix her hair and makeup. Dad needs his magazine time. After an extended visit Grandma leaves the toilet smelling like a waste treatment plant. Then you've got the older brother who bars you from the bathroom just to make you suffer. Your family of cats and dogs may have the same dynamics in play.

Many people believe cats are asocial creatures, but that's not entirely true. Wherever there is enough food for everyone, feral cats may establish colonies with flexible social structures. In these colonies, cats can join or leave at will. Mostly maturing males bail out, but occasionally females choose to bid adieu.

When food is scarce, natural cats divide into smaller groups or even go solo. They come together to mate, but the queen raises her kittens alone. These cats survive by chasing intruders away to preserve their resources. Whether male or female, the dominant cats get the food.

Bulletin on Bullies

Let me clarify something. I use the terms "bully" to describe the aggressor and victim for the target cat because behaviors are similar to school kids embroiled in schoolyard harassment. The behaviors may be similar, but likely not the motives. The feline bully is not a bad or mean cat; he's a feline prepper. He guards resources because he *needs* them—all of them. If the food bowl fails to magically refill tomorrow, he'll need every piece of kibble to survive. The litter box, favorite toys and even you are resources he needs to protect.

Micro-Territories

Whether inside or out, each kitty has a well-defined territory, built around a safe place called *home base*. An owned outside cat's home base probably consists of his yard and adjoining yards. It's the place where he hangs out most of the time and is willing to defend. A cat's home base may be a series of spots rather than a single location.

The cat's *home range* expands out from his home base. The size of a domestic cat's home range is always determined by the availability of food, shelter and water. How much land a kitty claims for home range also depends on the gender, neuter status and age. Because unaltered free-ranging males need room to hunt and locate eligible lady cats, they require the most turf.

At times a cat may choose to hang out with other friendly cats who share his home range. In more private moments, he may go into restricted areas of his home base where he doesn't have to associate with other kitties.

Domestic cats, whether they're innies or outies, timeshare overlapping territories. They are creatures of routine, and depend on a strict schedule to avoid direct conflict with another cat. Marking territory allows them to post information without coming face-to-face. (I talk about how cats use urine marking to communicate with other cats in Chapter 8 Cat Tagging: When Kitty Marks.)

Preferring to avoid a clash with another cat, an outside kitty will schedule their walks and choose convoluted routes through shared territory deliberately to bypass the interior territories of other cats so they don't have to encounter neighbors.

"Territoriality brings aggressive behavior. Both males and females tend to be aggressive toward intruders or strangers," Niels Pederson said. "One factor that keeps an animal's territory intact is its aggressive disposition toward other cats. That's why it is difficult, and sometimes impossible, for an adult cat in a household to accept new cats, even kittens. Many prefer to avoid each other, but if one intrudes into another's territory or if they are forced together, fighting can occur. If dominance is not established, they may remain intolerant of each other almost permanently."

The Kitty Hierarchy

Long before humans came up with vacation condos, cats invented the concept of timesharing. Like their outside counterparts, housecats have a flexible society. They also have overlapping territories and they time-share prime property.

There's real estate for every feline budget and personality. As with any community, some property is more valuable. You've got your premium properties, such as restaurant row (food bowls), sanitary facilities (litter boxes), penthouses (elevated shelves), fabulous views (window sills) and fitness centers (scratching posts). The value of a piece of property may depend on the time of day; a spot next to the window is more valuable when it's sun-soaked.

Feline hierarchy is not as clear-cut as in dogs. Cats display situational dominance, ruling the roost in specific locations and at specific times. One cat may be the dominant cat in the bedroom, while another is top cat in the living room. Hierarchies can also shift according to time of day and available resources.

A multicat study by Bernstein and Strack found that space within the household was not shared equally by all cats. Some kitties enjoyed greater access to resources than others. Another study by Knowles showed a connection between control of the food/water bowls and hostility around the house. Not surprisingly, food is the most common cause of conflict among inside cats. Cats may also openly or silently clash over litter boxes, perches, sunny areas, safe napping spots, elevated places where the cat can monitor his domain, or attention from their humans.

In a multicat house, a cat's home base may be very small—a windowsill, a specific shelf on the cat tree, or an individual cushion on the couch.

"You have Puffistan and Fluffistan," cat behavior consultant Beth Adelman explained. "Your house is like the former Yugoslavia, which is a small country now divided into even smaller countries. Each patch of area in your house is broken up into smaller countries. Each cat controls some countries. A specific cat's countries are very small, and they aren't contiguous. Even the couch can be divided into two or three countries." Perhaps Fluffy claims the east side of the sofa in the morning when the sun warms the cushions. Puff gets the other end and Tabby may occupy the elevated back of the couch. One cat may keep the others off the desk while you are working, but leave the desk as "free territory" when you are not in the room.

You might also look at your kitties the same way you'd look at the employees of a corporation. Expect to see the dominant cat occupying the high-rise real estate. He (or she) likes to be elevated so he can monitor what's happening in his realm. The Chief Cat Officer (CCO) gets the top-floor penthouse (the top shelf on the cat tree or the sunny spot on the recliner). As you drop down the corporate ladder, so do the offices. The mail clerk has his "office" in the basement with no windows (the lower arm of the cat tree), but it's still his domain. At the end of the day everyone goes home, the CCO to his mansion and the mail clerk to his apartment. The CCO drives a Mercedes, the clerk drives a Fiesta. They both have their territories—which are not contiguous—and they don't occupy a single spot all the time.

The difference between humans and cats is humans can become dissatisfied with their subjacent position. Cats, who are hardwired for a flexible hierarchy, don't. Adelman said cats are comfortable with a hierarchy even if they are on the lower end, "as long as all their needs are met. These needs include food and water, a safe place to go to the bathroom, affection and safety. When every cat gets what they need, you have peace."

Our Part in the Problem

When we humans bring multiple cats into our home, it's for *our* benefit, not our cats. Fluffy doesn't get to pick his friends, as he would if he were a feral cat. *You* pick his housemates. Because we dictate that our cats must live with two, or five, or even 10 other cats, who may or may not get along, we must understand that problems will crop up. It's irresponsible and even cruel to expect them to work it out on their own.

The difference between a feral cat community and an inside multicat home is when the going gets tough, inside kitties are stuck. Fluffy can't leave, no matter how much Buster busts his chops.

News flash: The more cats you have, the more likely you are to have marking and peeing problems. There's a connection between bickering among feline housemates and spraying. If you live with more than nine cats, there's a 100 percent chance that at least one kitty hoses the walls. Even in a one-cat home, there's still a 25 percent chance that a kitty will spray.

While conflict involving a new cat is easy to understand, conflict caused by a maturing cat is more puzzling. Although kitties may have lived peacefully for the first few years of their lives, between the ages of 2 and 5 years, cats reach social maturity. These newly mature kitties start to take some control of social groups and their activities, which may lead to open conflict within the clowder. A cat's perceptions of resource needs may expand when he reaches social maturity.

Redirected aggression

When Fluffy can't personally confront an animal who's invading his territory, redirected aggression may be the result. For example, two feline buddies are watching the birds through the window when an outside cat sprays the porch or a raccoon eats from the bird feeder. Fluffy can't rip the invader a new one because he's stuck behind that pesky pane of glass. So he does the next best thing: He smacks the cat sitting next to him. The poor victim cat, licking a sore nose, wonders, "What'd I do?" The victim could be the family dog or even you. (Learn what to do about outside provocateurs in Chapter 14: Outside Cats and Restraining Orders.)

Clandestine conflict

Conflict between kitties can either be in-your-face like rival gangs or secretive. In-your-face animosity involves stalking, hissing, chasing and demonstrations of the Halloween kitty stance to make the kitties look larger. Signs of clandestine conflict are so subtle you may not notice them—primarily blocking and staring.

The threatened kitty may avoid other cats, and/or become less active. He may even avoid human family members so he doesn't have to be around the cat who wants to (as we say in Texas) whoop his ass.

Other causes of aggression

When cats' perception of safety becomes threatened, they do what they must in order to regain that perception of control, including attacking or intimidating other kitties, withdrawing from the family or even becoming ill.

Conflicts can develop between longtime feline friends when a cat perceives a threat to his/her clowder status or rank by another inside cat or even a threat from outdoor intruders. Fear, anxiety and territorial disputes can contribute to intercat aggression.

Remember, as with inappropriate elimination, aggression could also be caused by pain or any number of illnesses, so when a normally calm cat turns aggressive, a trip to the vet is in order.

Other than illness, aggression could be triggered by a frightening event, or a change in the clowder's social structure (possibly caused by the death of a feline companion or the arrival of a new cat).

Telling the Bully from the Victim

The dominant cat does *not* stand next to the litter box with a sign that reads, "None shall pass." He'll lie on his side between the target and the litter box (or the food bowl), his back claws exposed, his eyes warning the victim not to approach. Those back claws are menacing weapons. Nobody wants a piece of that. Without raising a claw, Fluffy's body language blocks access. This causes the victim anxiety, even if there's no physical attack.

According to Dr. Karen L. Overall, a board certified applied animal behaviorist, cats who recognize each other as social equals are less likely to become physically aggressive toward each other. Instead, they may prevent others from using assets using subtle intimidation, such as pushing others away from food bowls, litter box ambushes, sneak attacks from hiding places, bluff charges and stealing favorite toys.

You can determine who's the bully by watching their eyes. The target cat won't make eye contact with his tormentor. But the bully need only lock eyes on the less confident cat to inspire fear. On the surface it looks so innocent. The chin slightly lowered, the eyelids squeezed together slightly. This isn't the "kitty kiss" we adore. It's a look so scorching the victim will abandon the bowls or the litter box. Or the bully may intimidate less confident cats by lowering his head and neck while raising his butt as he approaches them. He may even fluff up the fur on his back and tail, but not do the full Halloween kitty.

The assertive kitty is never intimidated by his victim and he will never retreat from the cat he's threatening. When the antagonistic cat is on the offense, he'll move closer to the other cats to control the encounter. As if in a dance routine, the threatened kitty will try to move away to increase the distance. Contrary to what most people believe, the victim cat is usually the one who hisses and shrieks, not the aggressor.

Because kitties don't have conflict resolution strategies or a clear-cut dominance hierarchy as dogs do, target kitties may try to avoid threatening encounters by hiding from other cats and the human family, staying in areas of the house that others do not use, or interacting with family members only when the bully isn't around. This isn't just a guy thing; when it comes to their little corner of the couch, females can act as territorial as the boys.

Although both offensive and defensive cats may soil the house, the target cat is more likely to spray or go outside the box. He will hide until his tormentor has left the room, coming out of his hiding place to eat and use the box. When a cat blocks the litter box, the victim must make other arrangements. After all, when you gotta go, you gotta go.

A cat who pees on beds, stoves, a potted plant or other elevated open places may do so because another cat is blocking the litter box or he's afraid he'll become trapped by another cat. "Because our cats evolved as both predator and prey, they need to feel safe when they are most vulnerable—eating, resting, eliminating," Dr. Buffington said. "If your cat feels threatened by anything in the environment, other pets, machinery, etc. when using the litter box, he may decide to eliminate somewhere that he feels safer!"

Cat owners may not notice such these subtle conflicts until the victim begins to hide, starts to hiss when he sees the bully, or develops a health problem Dr. Buffington said.

Threat can cause litter box mishaps too. This can occur both in cats with FIC (or Pandora Syndrome) and in healthy cats. Dr. Buffington has seen threatened male cats who spray bloody pee as a result of stress. (Read about this very complicated stress-induced illness in Feline Idiopathic Cystitis (Pandora Syndrome) in chapter 10.

A Box with a View

Fluffy needs a bathroom with a good view so he can see who's out there. He doesn't want to be ambushed by something lurking behind him while he's doing his business. In multicat households, cats want a litter box with an unobstructed view and an easy way to escape if they are confronted while in the box. Sometimes, even open boxes are wedged into corners or between things, where the cat feels hemmed in.

Tails from the Trenches

Judy Morgan DVM, CVA, CVCP, CVFT, a holistic vet from New Jersey, had a client whose cat refused to use the litter box. The box was situated out of the way behind a file cabinet, with no visibility. Turns out, the kitty's feline housemate launched surprise attacks when the victim cat was in the box. Dr. Morgan suggested moving the litter box out from behind the file cabinet into a position that offered a clear view of the doorway. Once the owner moved the bathroom, the cat started using the box again because he could watch the doorway to see if the bully cat was approaching.

Covered litter boxes

If you buy a hooded box to keep the dog from snacking out of the litter box, Fluffy may avoid the box. In a multipet home, bullied cats run the risk of becoming trapped inside a covered box by a more assertive cat or even the dog. Nobody wants to risk an ambush, cat behavior consultant Jennifer Mauger said. "Since the cat using the box can't see another cat coming, it can cause him to stop using a covered box. (Learn how to make a better covered litter box in Chapter 6 Make a More Acceptable Covered Box.)

Conflict Resolution

The best cure for territorial aggression and resource guarding is prevention. When you see aggressive posturing, separate the cats immediately. Each encounter reinforces their identities as bully and victim. "Our goal is to reduce unhealthy conflict to a more manageable level for cats involved," Dr. Buffington said. "The cat's perception of how much control it wants over the environment or its housemates' behaviors determines the result."

You need to set up an environment of plenty to introduce harmony to your multicat home (and hopefully stop or reduce the marking and litter box mishaps.) That means more territory and more resources.

While Herbert Hoover is credited with promising, "A chicken in every pot and a car in every garage," you should promise chicken cat food in every bowl and a litter box for every cat . . .plus one.

Break up your home into several different territories. The more territories, the less the cats are stressed. Create several separate spaces where they can hang out alone, so they can eat and go to the bathroom in peace.

The rule of paw is, you need one box per cat plus at least one extra. Some kitties prefer to pee in one place and poop in another, so you may need more than one box even if you have only one cat.

Although they're easier to maintain, don't simply cluster boxes side-by-side. This is your bully's dream come true. He can guard all four boxes with little or no effort. Scatter them in multiple locations throughout the house. Also place feeding stations and climbing places around the house in areas frequented by different cats. (Don't set the food right next to the litter box, because that's just yucky.) With resources spread in different locations, a target kitty can eat or go to the bathroom without having to encounter the bully. Adequate, yet safe, territory may reduce conflict to a tolerable level.

Increasing Territory

Cats need more space than the average house provides. To add more territory to your home, simply set up many desirable single-cat-size resting places. Create clever hiding places and hangouts in every room where the cats are allowed to go. Think in three dimensions. Cats are more comfortable living in groups if they can layer themselves. Since cats want to hang out high up, you can add elevated territory with tall cat trees, lofts, shelving units, wall-hung shelves, cat condos, and window perches. Simply remove the stuff from refrigerator tops, kitchen cabinet tops, counters or clear off cat-size spaces on several shelves of bookcases throughout the house. Set out cardboard boxes, paper bags (handles removed), hooded beds, baskets and carriers. These additional safe territories scattered around your home may reduce conflict and stress to a tolerable level. (See Chapter 13 Environmental Enrichment: Just What the Doctor Ordered for more territory expanding ideas).

Tails from the Trenches

Dr. Marci L. Koski, certified Feline Behavior and Training Professional, has five kitties. She placed all the recommended number of litter boxes in the basement where the family spent much of their free time. Suddenly, her cat Abbey started peeing in the upstairs bathroom and kitchen sinks. It progressed to her pooping right next to Marci's bed. There was nothing medically wrong with Abbey, so they started doing a little investigative work. It turns out that their other cat, Momo, was barring Abbey from the only entrance to the basement and the litter boxes! They immediately moved two of the litter boxes upstairs and the Abbey instantly began using them.

"This just underscores the need to have litter boxes in multiple locations in the home (and on every floor of the home), and have multiple access routes to the boxes," Dr. Koski said.

Why Not Try Reconciliation?

More serious social conflicts are treated by separating the feuding cats and slowly reintroducing them. You'll have to be the party planner here, arranging enjoyable situations that occur in each other's presence.

Completely separate the bully and the victim cat in two different rooms or areas of the house. At first, expect staring, hissing and/or growling from your bully if he walks by the target's sanctuary room. Ignore him. Don't yell. Give the bully his favorite treat whenever he's relaxed next to the sanctuary. At mealtime, feed them on opposite sides of the door so they can start to associate good things with the other cat. It's going to be hard, but they only get food, treats, attention and play in each other's company. Being with the other cat should be the best time of the day. Give them both lots of affection and playtime.

When everyone is calm, wedge the door open an inch or two with a door stop. Give both cats their favorite treats. The bully only gets a treat when he is relaxed. He gets nothing if he's fussing or staring at his target cat. Reward the target kitty for being brave. After the session, slide a rope dog toy, knotted at each end, under the door crack. Wiggle it around to encourage the cats to play together. Then—and here's the hard part— ignore them until the next session.

If that goes well and the bully is peaceful, next time open the door wider, around 4 inches. Reward good behavior. Give them treats and praise them whenever they are getting along.

Switch places. Allow the target kitty to go on a walkabout, while the bully eats in the sanctuary.

When the kitties can peacefully eat and play through the open door, it's time for a face-to-face reintroduction . . . from a distance.

On the day you want to introduce them face to face, lock the other pets away from the "dining" room and prepare two food bowls. Feed them on opposite ends of a large room at the same time. Return both kitties to their rooms. Each meal, move the bowls a little closer to each other.

If that goes well, you can double their pleasure by playing with both kitties at the same time with two cat tease toys such as ❀Da Bird (GO-CAT Feather Toys; Go-Cat.com; 517-543-7519), ❀Neko Birbug (Nekochan Enterprises, Inc.; Nekoflies.com; 866-699-6356) or ❀PURRfect™ Crunchy Feather Cat Toy (Vee Enterprises; VeeEnterprises.com; 800-733-1903.) Use two toys, one in each hand, allowing both cats to play in close quarters but not compete for the same toy. With you working the wands, you'll have your little predators jumping and running and snagging the toy—using up that predatory energy they'd otherwise use on you and the other cats. For the two feuding cats, fun times only happen when they are together. With each play session, increase their time together by a few minutes.

Let them associate for a longer period each excursion. Never "comfort" Buster for aggressive behavior (staring, hissing, stalking). Don't leave them alone until they can lie near each other comfortable and relaxed.

Break up squabbles immediately. Put the aggressor in the sanctuary. If either cat becomes aggressive or anxious, go back to the previous peaceful level of exposure.

Please don't try to speed up reintroduction. It may take a couple of months to change attitudes. Cutting corners will only exacerbate the problem. Whenever the cats involved in the conflict cannot be directly supervised, they may need to be separated. For example, the threatened cat could be provided with a refuge away from the other cats. This space should contain all necessary resources for the cat staying in it.

In severe situations, some cats may benefit from behavior-modifying medications. "In my experience, medication can help when combined with environmental enrichment, but cannot replace it," Dr. B said.

These feuding kitties may never be "best friends," but once they've been slowly reintroduced, they usually can live together without aggression or conflict-related illnesses. "They should cohabit," Dr. Ogata said. "Our goal is to make them roommates, not a married couple. Nice neighbors."

When slow reintroductions don't work, you may need to create totally separate territories, so they don't have to come in contact with each other. Think screen door. Each room should contain all necessary resources for the cat staying in it.

New Cat Introductions

Open conflicts are most common when a new cat moves into a home with resident cats. Suddenly, a stable society has a new kitty jockeying for status. It can throw the entire clowder into chaos. Let the spraying begin!

If you take the time to gradually introduce a newcomer to your existing feline family, you won't have to act as a full-time referee. As with humans, proper introductions go a long way toward building a lifelong friendship, or at the least, cats that can tolerate each other.

Since a new cat doesn't automatically know where to find the litter box, don't let Newman run amok. Prepare a quiet sanctuary and let him get used to the sights, smells, people and other pets slowly. Set up his litter box and food bowl in opposite corners of a bathroom or other quiet small room, plus toys and a scratching post. Let him relax there for a week or two to acclimate to his environment. This gives him time to learn where the box is. Let him rehearse the behavior before letting him run free in your home. (Use the reintroduction instructions in the section above.)

Other things that help tame the beast include:
• Regular individual exercise with a tease toy.
• Bell that bully so the target kitty can get advance notice when he approaches, reducing the opportunity for an ambush. Early warning will give other kitties the chance to get out of the path of the storm. (This

doesn't always work. Some bullies have been to charm school and can walk smoothly without ringing the bell.)

When the tension grows so thick you can cut it, separate the feuding parties. You can also use ❧Comfort Zone with Feliway® MultiCat (PetComfortZone.com) to inspire friendlier interaction. This diffuser uses an analogue of the calming pheromones produced by lactating queens.

Canine Conflict

To a kitty, the important thing is a concept of safety. *You* know Fluffy is safe inside your home, but he's not so sure. Not to beat a dead rat, but kitties are fierce little predators, but they're also prey for larger carnivores, including dogs.

You trust that Fideaux would never harm a follicle on Fluffy's body, but from Fluffy's perspective, he may be sleeping with the enemy and might be at risk of being reclassified as a main course at any moment. If you want to learn all about canine-feline relationships, read Arden Moore's book, *Fit Dog: Tips and Tricks to Give Your Pet a Longer, Healthier, Happier Life*, especially chapter 9 and Amy D. Shojai's, *ComPETability: Solving Behavior Problems in Your CAT-DOG Household.*

Always make sure the cat has an elevated escape place, so he can get away from the dog if he feels threatened.

That *perception* of untrustworthy companionship isn't reserved strictly for the family dog; it could extend to other cats, kids and even you. Well intentioned rough play may appear to Fluffy as a predatory threat.

(If you need more detailed information about living in a multicat family, I devoted my entire book *Cat Wrangling Made Easy: Maintaining Peace and Sanity in Your Multicat Home* to the topic.)

10 SO SICK IT'S CRIMINAL: FELINE LOWER URINARY TRACT DISEASE

Inappropriate elimination is actually inappropriate communication.
~Dusty Rainbolt

Disclaimer: Please remember, this book is not intended to be a substitute for professional veterinary advice, diagnosis or treatment for your cat. Hopefully, these three chapters on medical issues will help you understand and empathize with your cat's condition and seek treatment. Contact your veterinarian if you have any questions regarding your cat's health. If you notice a change in your cat's behavior, take him to the vet to rule out any underlying medical causes.

Peeing outside the litter box is a common sign of feline lower urinary tract disease (FLUTD). According to a 2005 (and subsequent) report published by Veterinary Pet Insurance Co., FLUTD was the most common reason owners took their cats to a vet. In 2015, 5 percent of all cat claims at Trupanion pet insurance were for lower urinary tract problems including: feline idiopathic cystitis or inappropriate elimination. Male cats accounted for 53 percent of those claims.

Veterinarians have been writing about lower urinary tract disorders in indoor cats for more than eight decades. Through the years, the names of conditions describing bloody, painful, frequent urination have changed: urinary tract infections, feline urologic syndrome (FUS) and feline lower urinary tract disease (FLUTD). These name changes reflect our changing understanding of the problem.

FLUTD isn't a single disease; it's an umbrella term like cancer or infection) used to describe a number of painful conditions that affect a kitty's bladder and urethra. It can be caused by:
- Feline idiopathic cystitis (FIC), a stress-induced disease
- Bladder stones or crystals
- Bacterial infection
- Urethral plugs or other obstructions
- Trauma
- Cancer of the bladder
- Anatomical abnormalities

Because FLUTD has so many possible causes, it can be challenging to diagnose the particular cause in any particular case. All conditions under the FLUTD umbrella can cause pain and a persistent urge to urinate. While the underlying cause of FLUTD can vary from cat to cat, kitties can exhibit some or all of these signs:
- Peeing outside the box
- Straining to pee
- Repeatedly squatting in the box with little results
- No evidence of having peed at all (If he's squatting but passing no pee, your cat is experiencing a urinary tract obstruction. This is a life-threatening emergency. Go to the vet immediately.)
- Passing bloody pee
- Crying out while squatting to pee
- Peeing in different locations
- Showing a preference for smooth, cool surfaces like bathtubs or tile floors
- Frequently licking his private parts
- Vomiting
- Lethargy

Let's try to get into your cat's head for a moment. If it hurts while he's standing in the litter box, then in the words of Mr. Spock, feline logic dictates that he pee someplace where it doesn't hurt him, such as behind the couch or in a bathroom sink. Unfortunately, that strategy doesn't work so well. That darn bladder pain follows Fluffy no matter where he pees. So he continues to seek out new corners and new elimination places—to boldly go where no cat has gone before. Relieving himself in an inappropriate place is as close as he can come to texting you, "Help me. I feel like poop." You should accommodate him and take him on a car trek to the vet.

Your vet will examine your cat, check his blood pressure, and may run bloodwork, urinalysis and urine culture, and/or take X-rays (to check for stones, foreign bodies and physical abnormalities).

Risk Factors

In his proceedings, "Feline idiopathic cystitis: Epidemiology, risk factors and pathogenesis," presented at the Hill's Global Symposium on Feline Lower Urinary Tract Health in Prague, 2014, Dr. Andy Sparkes reported that the Persian (especially Himalayans) and Manx breeds had a greater risk of developing FLUTD. Lucky Siamese had a reduced risk. Moving to a new home or adding another cat to the house can increase the odds of developing FLUTD.

Dr. Dru Forrester, in her proceedings from the 2007 Hill's FLUTD Symposium revealed the typical FLUTD cat is:
• Middle-aged (4 to 7-years-old)
• Neutered
• Lives inside
• Expected to toilet in a litter box
• Lives with at least one other cat
• Eats dry food
• Experiences disruptions in daily routine
• Overweight
• Gets little exercise

Increasing Water Intake

Switching your cat's diet from dry to canned food, or adding water or broth to kibble helps dilute a cat's pee. (Don't worry about the "benefit" of dry food keeping your cat's teeth clean. It's another myth, according to Dr. Buffington.)

You can encourage additional water consumption by adding low-sodium broth to cat food, providing a cat drinking fountain, switching from a plastic bowl to ceramic, changing the water a couple of times a day, allowing the cat to drink from the running faucet, or by adding meat or fish-flavored ice cubes to his water. (I offer more suggestions in Chapter 13 Environmental Enrichment: Just What the Doctor Ordered.)

Urinary Tract Infection (UTI)

For years most cats with bloody urine were thought to have bacterial bladder or urinary tract infections (UTI), but in reality, only 1 to 3 percent of FLUTD cats are diagnosed with UTIs. Bona fide UTIs are caused by bacteria, fungus, virus, or can be a byproduct of crystals and stones. We now know that bladder infections rarely occur in cats under the age of 10.

A urinalysis and urine culture will show the presence of bacteria. It is treated with a round of antibiotics.

Feline Idiopathic Cystitis (Pandora Syndrome)

The most common single cause of FLUTD is feline idiopathic cystitis (FIC). FIC is the technical term for chronic urinary tract problems without a known cause. In two-thirds of cases when the cat is peeing blood, straining to pee and repeatedly trying to use the litter box, vets can't find a cause. That's when they default to a diagnosis of FIC. (They used to call it feline *interstitial* cystitis, but that's so 2010.)

Typically, FIC kitties have no bacteria in their pee, so antibiotics won't help. About 85 percent of the time FIC symptoms disappear within a week, whether kitty receives medicine or not, but a whopping 50 percent of those same kitties will experience another episode within a year, according to Dr. Buffington.

FIC is associated with inside confinement, lack of physical activity, obesity, arthritis, and other environmental and health issues. Believe it or not, FIC can also be caused by dirty litter boxes, boxes placed in bad locations, as well as not enough litter boxes.

Diagnosing FIC

There's no test that can definitively identify FIC. Vets diagnose it by the (pardon the pun) process of elimination. Your vet will give your kitty a physical examination, and will most likely order X-rays, urinalysis and a urine culture. After other diseases (including crystals and stones, urinary tract obstructions, anatomic abnormalities and bladder infections) are ruled out, that leaves FIC.

How FIC affects kitties

Cats affected by FIC tend to be uneasy little head cases, more fearful and nervous than other cats in the same home. Studies show they aren't as active as the other kitties. They don't play "hunt," and they drink less water than the healthy cats. Not only does the FIC cat's urinary tract hurt, he probably feels lousy all over. Dr. Buffington and other researchers think chronic FIC is part of a general response to threat that can also include other body systems. From this view, the bladder is one victim, rather than the perpetrator of an underlying problem. It's a systemic disorder associated with an overly sensitive stress response system, rather than a bladder-specific problem, which can affect almost any part of the body. FIC has been linked through overactivity of the stress response system to nervous system, hormonal and immune changes, as well as heart, lung, digestive tract, respiratory, nervous system, and skin problems. So a kitty who suffers from FIC might also have itchy skin, painful mouth inflammation or digestive issues—another reason why he's too "lazy" to hike to the basement to use the litter box. Signs from these other organ systems may wax and wane in intensity and frequency, just like cystitis signs do.

Dr. Buffington, who has researched FIC for many years, coined the phrase "Pandora Syndrome" to describe cats with multiple health and behavior problems resulting from chronic stress. Pandora refers to this larger multiorgan disorder, because it's similar to the troubles that escaped from Pandora's mythical box.

The stress response system of Pandora Syndrome cats appears to be unusually sensitive, due to exposure to a strong threat very early in life, maybe even before birth. When the stress response system is too active, damage can also occur to other organs.

In addition to peeing outside the box, Pandora kitties may exhibit any number of "sickness behaviors", including vomiting, diarrhea, loss of appetite, decreased water intake, fever, lethargy, painful behaviors, decreased activity, and failure to groom and socialize.

"The bladder isn't the cause of the problem," Dr. B said. "It's the victim of the problem. FIC is like a migraine. Imagine it's a migraine affecting the bladder." There's no real cure, but its effects can be mitigated by stress management.

As with the Pandora myth hope remains.

FIC risk factors

A typical FIC cat is an obese couch potato under 10 years old. He lives indoors with at least one other cat. He must relieve himself in a (possibly dirty) litter box rather than going outside, and eats mostly dry food. He's unusually stressed by his environment and often suffers from other medical conditions. At least two studies point to dry cat food as a contributing risk factor of FIC, although other studies have found that cats can recover without changing the diet.

Veterinary researchers have noticed similarities between FIC and the human bladder condition (often affecting women) called interstitial cystitis. Dr. Buffington said it's as close to the same disease in different species as you can get.

I can personally attest that interstitial cystitis truly sucks. You have the constant urge to pee, whether your bladder is full or not. When you attempt to go, it feels like you're trying to expel a kitchen knife. Cats with FIC probably experience something similar. Researchers associate human interstitial cystitis with environmental stress. Stress also appears to be a factor in FIC in cats.

Stress

"Nonspecific irritation of the bladder lining is often caused by a change in the pH of the urine," Dr. Levitan said. "Clinical studies show that stress alone can change the pH of a cat's urine."

Stress is an organism's response to any demand. When faced with a fight-or-flight emergency, the body releases nerve chemicals and hormones that quicken the pulse and respiration, and cause the muscles to tense. These metabolic changes help an animal either confront the threat or run away, improving his chance of surviving. But these same chemicals, released for a prolonged period, lead to health problems.

According to Dr. Buffington, a chemical reaction occurs in the brain when a cat perceives his environment as stressful. Unfortunately, in FIC cats, the brain chemical that stops the stress response is limited, so the response persists. Chronic stress can eventually result in tissue damage and disease.

In humans, chronic stress can cause heart disease, high blood pressure, immune disorders, digestion issues, diabetes and depression, as well as bladder lining irritation. Chronic stress can affect your cat the same way.

Stress—seriously? Your cat sleeps 16 hours a day and has access to 24/7 room service. He doesn't have to worry about eating or being eaten. What could possibly stress him? Surprisingly, almost everything.

While you can take your feline out of the wilderness, you can't take the wilderness out of your feline. Despite your protective walls, Fluffy still worries about falling prey to larger predators and protecting his personal territory. He constantly assesses risk and looks for danger. And in his mind, danger is everywhere.

Cats are creatures of habit. Any change in his environment can generate stress because it could foreshadow a threat. Also because your cat's senses are much more acute than yours, sounds, smells and textures that you find pleasing—or at least inoffensive—may overwhelm him.

Without even realizing it, we humans can create a stressful environment for our cats. For example, we often force our kitties to live with other hostile feline companions, and/or a cat's primary predator–dogs. (Think about that. In the wild, canines eat cats. How disturbing must it be for a timid cat to share a water bowl with a German Shepherd?) Many of the factors that contribute to increased stress also have to do with living indoors exclusively.

Unfortunately signs of stress are also the same behaviors you'll observe connected to almost any disease mentioned in this book. They include:

- **Urine marking/peeing or pooping outside the litter box**
- **Defensive or redirected aggression toward people or other pets**
- **Changes in appetite**: Eating more, loss of appetite or not eating at all
- **Changes in grooming habits**: Excessive grooming, which may cause bald spots, or under grooming resulting in matted or spiky-looking fur
- **Isolation**: Hiding, your cat spends less time with family than usual or no longer hangs out with other pets
- **Excessive scratching or itchiness**
- **Changes in activity level**: Suddenly quiet or lethargic, or extreme vigilance, startling at the slightest noise.

Things that cause stress to cats include:
- **Conflict with other cats or pets**: Even contagious illnesses passed back and forth between feline housemates play a role in increasing stress
- **Not enough territory**: No place to hide, lack of elevated spots to get away from kids or other pets
- **Lack of resources or inability to get to food or litter box**: Multiple food and water bowls or litter boxes located side by side only count as one, because other pets can easily guard all the resources at once.
- **Neighbor pet or wild animals in the yard**
- **Problems with the litter box**: Unscooped or dirty litter boxes, scented litter, a new brand of litter, a covered box, a new location, laundry room or air vent noise, another pet or child interfering with using the box. "Anything that hampers litter box use may increase the time the cat retains urine between eliminations," Dr. Buffington says. The longer a compromised bladder wall holds pee the more the bladder lining will become inflamed. Ouch
- **Any recent change in the environment**: Even something as insignificant (to you) as a new bedspread
- **Change in family**: Arrival of new baby, pet, spouse, roommate or of significant other; absence or *loss* of family member due to hospitalization, death, breakup, kids leaving for college or camp, or death or illness of another pet

• **Family conflict**: Fighting between family members, child, spousal or animal abuse, cat bullied by kids or other pets

• **A move to a new home**: Kitties who have recently moved may experience stress for up to three months

• **Loud or violent weather**: Rain and winter weather can stress cats for as long as a month

• **Earthquakes and other natural disasters**

• **Loud music or noise**

• **Strangers in the home**: Houseguests, pet sitters, trick or treaters, birthday parties, etc.

• **Food**: Switching cat food brand, flavor or texture, not enough bowls, dishes clustered in one area or food dishes located near the litter box

• **Home remodeling**: New carpet, rearranged or new furniture, construction, painting, or home repairs

• **Schedule disruption**: New job and work hours, house guests arrive so feeding and litter box cleaning times change, schedule changes due to Daylight Savings Time

• **Illness or injury**

• **Travel**: Traveling with owners or going to a boarding kennel, the owner traveling or a pet sitter coming to the house

FIC treatment through environmental enrichment

"To know all is to forgive all, not to excuse all," Dr. B said about FIC. "You can predict it if the kitten comes from a stressful situation. You can prevent it from the moment the cat enters the home. It's not hard. This is an animal reacting to the environment."

We humans are used to taking an aspirin to banish a headache or antibiotics to kill an infection. It would be nice to medicate your cat's way to bladder tranquility, but a magic pill for FIC is as mythical as Pandora herself. FIC outbreaks usually resolve within a couple of weeks with or without treatment, so most treatment programs provide pain relief and stress reduction, as well as attempt to prevent future episodes.

Because you don't want your cat to feel like he's peeing a dagger, talk to your vet about providing pain relief during FIC episodes. She may prescribe butorphanol or meloxicam to make your kitty more comfortable.

When it comes to addressing Pandora Syndrome, Dr. Buffington said you need to treat the source, not just the symptoms. "Cats are so misunderstood," he said.

Dr. Buffington's research has shown that FIC symptoms, fearfulness, nervousness and other stress-related sickness behaviors improved by 75 to 80 percent when the cat's environment was predictable: they were fed at the same time, the litter boxes were cleaned on schedule and left in place, and handlers regularly played with the cats.

When you arrange a predictable and enriching environment, you not only give your cat all the resources he needs (food, water, litter boxes), and reduce conflict with other cats, you mimic the opportunity and lifestyles your cat would have in the wild. (Check out Chapter 13 Environmental Enrichment: Just What the Doctor Ordered.)

Tails from the Trenches

Jennifer from Arizona had a cat named Kitty, who developed cystitis. Kitty peed everywhere *but* the litter box. The vet explained Kitty had formed a pain association with the litter box—every time she stepped into the box to pee, she experienced pain—so she constantly looked for a safe place to go. Her favorite locations were Jennifer's bed and laundry. Jennifer bought 30 disposable baking dishes, filled them with litter, and left them all over the house. The kitty would use a different pan each time, until her pain meds started working and she no longer associated pain with the litter box. Eventually Jennifer started removing the throwaway pans, and Kitty returned to her litter box, which Jennifer had rotated in a different direction, so that it appeared "new."

Stress, exercise and play

Dr. Buffington found that having access to outdoor prey actually reduced a cat's stress, the same way that participation in sports has a stress-relieving effect on people. So vigorous play, a couple of times a day, will help with your kitty's stress issues.

Did you know that the National Institute of Mental Health recommends people exercise 30 minutes per day to boost mood and reduce stress? The organization also urges scheduling regular times for healthy and relaxing activities.

The same is good for your kitty. Fluffy doesn't need 30 minutes of activity. Since few kitties voluntarily hop on a treadmill, cat-isthenics take the form of old-fashioned playtime. Just two 10-minute rounds of Kill the Feather, or whatever both you and your cat enjoy, will reduce your cat's, and possibly your, stress.

Human-operated interactive toys will give Fluffy the thrill of hunting prey. These toys encourage Fluffy to run around and pounce. Play with feather toys and lures on a stick until he's too tired to move. You may have to experiment to discover the toy that turns him on. Some of my cats' favorite interactive toys that stimulate hunting behavior are:

- Da Bird
- Neko Birbug
- Vee Enterprises PURRfect™ FeatherBouncer
- Cat Charmer (Cat Charmer; Cat Dancer Products®, Inc. CatDancer.com; 800-844-6369)

There's a real reason why Dr. Dodman frequently says, "A tired cat is a good cat." He was the director of the behavior clinic at the Cummings School of Veterinary Medicine at Tufts University. "Exercise increases serotonin in both humans and cats," Dr. Dodman said. "Serotonin is found in Prozac. Low serotonin levels in our furry friends produce irritability, increase aggression and cause depression. Higher serotonin levels promote feelings of well-being and self-confidence."

L-theanine supplements

An uncontrolled clinical study appearing in the *Journal of Veterinary Behavior* (May-June 2007) reported that the natural supplement, L-theanine, (Anxitane®, Virbac) reduces signs of anxiety in cats, including inappropriate elimination, fear, aggression, multipet problems, and physical manifestations of anxiety. The ideal dose is 25 mg twice each day (50 mg total per day). There are also other brands of L-theanine including Composure chewable treats by Vetri-science, Pet Naturals Calming for Cats, and GNC Ultra Mega Relax for Cats. Check the label dosing instructions. You can also buy the L-theanine capsules for humans. (Make sure capsules contain no other ingredients besides L-theanine.) Human supplements typically come in 100 mg capsules. Open the capsule, divide the powder into two 50 mg portions, and mix the powder in with the cat's food once a day. Contents of one capsule will last 2 days.

Pheromones

Dr. Buffington encourages cat owners to try synthetic feline facial pheromones in addition to other environmental enrichment efforts. Some studies have shown that synthetic calming pheromones may help decrease stress. ❀Comfort Zone with Feliway is a synthetic facial pheromone that comes in a pump spray and plug-in diffuser. In a 2004 double-blind, placebo-controlled study of cats with recurrent FIC, the owners of more than half the cats whose environment was treated daily with Feliway for two months said their cats' clinical signs and behavior improved, and they experienced a reduced number of cystitis episodes. The study appeared in the Journal of Feline Medicine and Surgery. While I'm unaware of studies, ❀SENTRY® Calming Spray for Cats utilizes a synthetic pheromone produced by lactating mother cats. The Sentry pheromones come infused in a collar, as well as in a pump spray or diffuser. I've found the ❀SENTRY Calming Collar helped relieve anxiety in some cats in areas too large to effectively use plug-ins and sprays.

Stress medication

If environmental modification doesn't help Fluffy with his symptoms, your vet may prescribe anti-anxiety meds. Dr. Buffington's study recommends treating FIC pain flare-ups with acepromazine and buprenorphine. Amitriptyline can help kitty cope with stress, but veterinarians disagree how long a cat can stay on this medication. Your vet will need to monitor your cat's blood platelets, white blood cell count and liver enzymes while Fluffy is on the medication.

Unfortunately, Dr. Buffington's research found that glucosamine and pentosan polysulfate—once touted for an ability to coat the lining of the bladder and soothe irritation—were ineffective for FIC cats.

As mentioned, the signs tend to go away in cats within a few days regardless of treatment. Because veterinarians most commonly see cats when they are having signs, they may confuse the effects of their treatment with the natural course of the signs. This is why so many treatments thought to work based on clinical observation fail when subjected to properly conducted clinical trials.

Reducing stress through environmental enrichment

Since stress brings on so many health issues that contribute to inappropriate elimination, here are some easy changes you can make around the house to improve Fluffy's physical and mental state.

• A pleasing litter box. Dr. Tony Buffington said one element of environmental enrichment is a clean, easily accessible litter box. You need an adequate number of litter boxes to serve your kitties. The rule of paw is one litter box for every cat, plus one. They should be located in safe, easy-to-get-to places in the area your cat hangs out. Boxes should be clean, scooped at least once a day and changed when litter smells musty. (For more on what your cat expects from his litter box read Chapter 6 Thinking Inside the Litter Box.)

• Adequate resources. Fresh food and water stations, scratching posts and toys, distributed in safe locations throughout the house rather than one centralized one location.

• Increase special one-on-one time with your kitty. If he enjoys it, massage or brush him while you're watching TV. The DVD, ❀*Cat Massage* by Maryjean Ballner, can give you a few pointers to keep Fluffy coming back for more. ❀Zoom Groom is a massaging cat brush.

• Offer the chance to express natural predatory behaviors. Climbing

posts or opportunities to hunt lifelike prey
- Scheduled playtime
- Provide plenty of territory. Create hidey holes, elevated hang outs, and climbing platforms, window perches and cat trees so he can escape unwanted attention from kids or dogs. Provide multiple safe hiding places like boxes, enclosed baskets and even paper shopping bags (with the handles removed) so your cat can have a little "me time" away from other pets (and kids).
- Offer food puzzles, cat toys, cat grass and cat videos
- Keep changes to a minimum. If you must change his food or litter, do it gradually, and always offer changes as choices.
- Scheduled dining. Automatic pet feeder and pet feeding apps allow you to automatically feed Fluffy on a schedule. Will a change in diet help? Maybe. Dr. Buffington says, "While there is no nutrient or ingredient that is known to be therapeutic (by me anyway), the hedonic (smell, taste, mouth feel) properties of the food may be important to some cats. One also can consider all aspects of feeding management (timing, location, vehicle), which also may be helpful."
- Horizontal and vertical scratching surfaces
- Scheduled playtime

Diet

Dr. Buffington adds that while researchers have found no nutrient or ingredient that combats FIC, diet still plays a role in the disease. When switching a cat's food, do it gradually. "Don't take the old food away," Dr. B warns. "Don't mix it. Offer them side by side."

If you take away the old diet, you're increasing your cat's stress and he may simply refuse to eat. That potentially creates a whole new set of problems; not eating can result in life-threatening hepatic lipidosis, also called fatty liver disease. Provide his regular food and set out a bowl of the wet diet next to it. As Fluffy starts to eat the moist food, you can gradually reduce the dry food.

Cats aren't designed to eat a single large meal, so divide Fluffy's daily ration into two or three smaller meals.

"It has to do with feeding a cat a diet he wants in the way he wants to eat," Dr. B said. "The diet itself could be a stressor."

Dr. B recommends feeding kitties out of a food puzzle. Food puzzles are food dispensing toys that provide mental stimulation because they require kitties to figure out the trick to getting a meal. (I discuss food puzzles in Natural Eating Opportunities in Chapter 13.) "It's the difference between static and dynamic in dining."

Think about where you are feeding him as well. Cats are most vulnerable when they're eating, sleeping and eliminating.

Bladder Stones and Crystals

Bladder stones and crystals can form inside the bladder, causing inflammation of the bladder and urethra. These crystals can mingle with minerals, mucus, and other debris to form plugs that block the urethra. This is a serious, painful—and potentially fatal—condition.

Bladder stones and crystals account for 15 to 23 percent of FLUTD cases according to Dr. Forrester. These rock-hard mineral formations are a pain in the privates, particularly in male cats.

Tails from the Trenches

A client brought a 4-year-old gray cat named Smokey to Dr. Drew Weigner's clinic, The Cat Doctor in Atlanta. "She'd been peeing all over the house for six months," the woman told Dr. Weigner. "Fix this cat or put it to sleep." Dr. Weigner found blood in the urine and an X-ray showed a very faint bladder stone. Two days after surgery to remove the stone, Smokey began using the litter box again.

Diet, dry food, not drinking enough water and heredity can contribute to the formation of crystals and stones. It was once believed that too much ash and magnesium in cat food caused bladder crystals and stones, but current thought ties it to the pH of the food.

The treatment your vet chooses will depend on the stones' mineral composition. While there are many types of bladder stones, struvite and calcium oxalate are the most common.

Your vet may prescribe a stone-dissolving diet to combat struvite stones. If that doesn't do the trick, or if the stone has grown too large to either dissolve or pass, surgery will be necessary to remove it. Struvite stones aren't as common as they once were because most cat food formulas have reduced the proportion of magnesium and added acid to foods to cut down on the chance of struvite formation.

Calcium oxalate, the other likely mineral contender, can't be dissolved with diet. If the stones are small enough your vet may be able to flush them from the bladder; if the stone is too large to pass, it's back to surgery.

Cats who have been treated for stones run the risk of a relapse. After treating the initial problem, your vet will probably switch your cat to a bladder-friendly diet, and maybe even canned food. Your vet may also prescribe medication and a wet diet and/or supplement to prevent a recurrence.

Proper hydration is important for cats predisposed to stones. Water dilutes the concentration of the pee and reduces the chance that crystals will form, so make sure your cat has access to fresh, clean water at all times.

Obstructions

[WARNING!] The most serious FLUTD problem is an obstruction of the urethra, the tube that drains urine from bladder and out (hopefully) into the litter box. Obstructions happen far more often in male cats than in females. In addition to becoming blocked by stones or plugs, the urethra also can be blocked by spasms of the muscles surrounding the urethra.

When kitty can no longer pass pee, his kidneys stop filtering toxins from his blood. If the blockage isn't addressed, the cat will eventually lose consciousness. Left untreated, a fully obstructed cat who is otherwise healthy *will* die within 48 hours. A cat with kidney disease or other health issue may last 24 hours. [WARNING!]A partial or total blockage of the urethra is a *life-threatening* emergency that requires immediate veterinary intervention. An obstructed cat can't wait until the morning. It's an excruciating way to go.

Signs of an obstruction include frequent attempts to pee but producing only drops or no pee at all, straining to pee, and possibly crying out in pain while trying to pee. As the cat becomes more critical he'll become lethargic.

Under general anesthesia the vet will run a narrow tube called a catheter through the urethra and into the bladder allowing the urine to flow out. Some cats experience repeated obstruction episodes. In those cases the vet may suggest a perineal urethrostomy that changes Henry into Henrietta.

Crystals, stones and plugs

Bladder stones and crystals are a common cause of bladder and urethral obstruction. (In a 1997 study, anatomic anomalies were found in around 10 percent of all FLUTD cases.) Urinalysis, X-rays and/or ultrasound will help your vet diagnose the presence of stones or crystals.

Crystals can mingle with dead cells, mucus and other debris floating around in the bladder, forming a plug. As the plug moves from the bladder to the urethra it can become caught in the tube and creates a blockage that prevents Fluffy from emptying his bladder.

After removing the plug, your vet will probably switch your cat to a bladder friendly diet, and maybe even canned food.

Behavior Disorders

Inappropriate elimination is a vicious cycle. What started as a medical issue can, over time, turn into a behavioral problem, and vice versa. In one study of 100 cats with litter box problems, over one-third of the cats had a history of FLUTD. Vets diagnose a cat with a behavior disorder after excluding all medical causes.

Prevention and Home Monitoring

You can monitor the output of a kitty with diagnostic cat litters and dipsticks. This doesn't replace having your vet regularly test your cat's bodily fluids, but you can keep tabs on kitty's condition between vet visits.

You can obtain stress-free urine samples by putting Fluffy in lockup temporarily. Preferably the room has a hard floor, so he's not tempted to pee outside the box. Replace his regular cat litter with washed fine aquarium gravel, unpopped popcorn kernels or a non-absorbing cat litter such as ❀Kit4Cat Hydrophobic Sand and ❀Kit4Cat Cat Urine Sample Collection Kit (Coastline Global; Kit4Kat.com; 888-999-3050.) None of these absorb moisture, so the pee will form puddles. Pull the sample out with a clean syringe (minus the needle—you can get one from your vet), refrigerate it, and hand it over to your vet. Between vet visits you can use ❀Reagent test strips to check for pH, glucose or the presence of blood. (Get Reagent strips from your vet or Amazon.com.) With the pee pooled in this "litter," you can use the test strips to alert you to the presence of blood caused by inflammation or a change in pH. ❀CheckUp at home wellness test for cats comes complete with Kit4Cat Hydrophobic sand, collector kit and testing strips for blood, protein, glucose levels and pH. (CoastlineGlobal.com.)

Testing strips may show a false positive or a false negative. Keep an eye on your cat for signs of illness and test again the next time he pees or the next day. It's better to err on the side of caution, Dr. Rigoni said.

If you don't need a sterile sample, drill holes in a new plastic litter box and set that box inside an identical litter box. When the cat pees, the urine will flow into the bottom box. Use a new syringe to draw the sample out of the box. Take it to your vet.

An option to monitor for blood is to use a clear or white silica gel litter ❀Dr. Elsey's Senior, ❀Crystal Clear Litter Pearls (Ultra PET®; UltraPet.com; 864-261-3546), which allows you to see pink-tinged pee spots if your cat's pee contains blood caused by inflammation or crystals.

❀Dr. Elsey's Health Monitor™ Everyday Litter (Precious Cat Products; PreciousCat.com; 877-311-2287) is a consistent particle-size scoopable litter that will help you monitor kidney function, diabetes and hyperthyroidism in your cat. Once a month weigh your cat's pee clump. Because the grain size is calibrated, a change in the weight of the clump may be a sign of kidney or thyroid disease or diabetes.

"Honey, I think the Cat Just spelled SOS!"

11 SO SICK IT'S CRIMINAL: EVERYTHING ELSE

Personally, I have always felt the best doctor in the world is the veterinarian.
He can't ask his patients what's the matter. He's just got to know.
~ Will Rogers

Not to beat a dead rat, but when a well-mannered cat suddenly starts avoiding the litter box, he's not committing a crime, he's broadcasting an

SOS. If you don't understand Morris Code, take him to the vet. Don't assume he's misbehaving or peeing on the carpet out of spite. Unlike your 5-year-old kid, Fluffy can't tell you he feels sick. Instead, cats suffer in silence and offer you hints in the form of behavior changes.

Tails from the Trenches

Tank was a 4-year old strapping brown tabby who found himself at animal control after his owner died. I rescued Tank and his brother, fostering them at my house for a month or so. Outgoing, happy and well-behaved, they were quickly adopted together. Six months after moving into their new home, Tank started pooping in the couple's bathtub. I instructed them to take him to the vet. They claimed they already had, and that the vet said Tank was "fine." (I didn't believe that for a moment.) They returned the boys to me. Bloodwork showed Tank was actually in end-stage liver failure. He didn't make it. If the couple had really taken him to the vet when he first started pooping in the tub, Tank might have survived. Tank was telling them in the only way he could that he felt sick.

Cats are complicated little animals who deserve an A-Cat-emy Award for Best Portrayal of a Healthy Lifeform. In the wild, a sick or injured cat's middle name is "Appetizer." Guess what would happen if a feral cat carried on, "Oh, my tummy hurts. Won't someone help me?" Every coyote and stray dog within five miles would invite Fluffy to dinner—as the main course. As a survival strategy, cats hide illness until they're too sick to conceal the symptoms. When a normally well-mannered cat, like Tank, suddenly strays from the litter box, he's sending you a medical SOS.

"People believe inappropriate elimination is [a] behavioral [issue] all the time," Dr. Drew Weigner said. Dr. Weigner is a board-certified feline specialist and owner of The Cat Doctor in Atlanta. "[Look for] subtle changes like peeing outside the box and sleeping someplace different. By the time you see [medical] symptoms, cats are usually very sick. At that point you're practicing crisis medicine. Preventive medicine is when you first notice early changes."

"It's so simple to find out through a urinalysis (UA). If there's a medical problem, the UA won't be normal. If you have a cat peeing outside the box and the UA absolutely normal, it's behavioral."

Dr. Weigner said inflammation will show "more red blood cells and possibly some white blood cells" in the urine. A urinalysis may also reveal an altered pH, blood, pus, excessive protein, crystal sediment and other fascinating stuff.

Even if Fluffy has been to the vet recently, take him back. Health-wise, things can change rapidly. Just because he was healthy three weeks (or even three days) ago doesn't mean he's OK today. When *you* catch a stomach bug, you're fine one day and sick the next. Your kitty may have been fine on his last vet visit, but he's feeling rotten now. He may have actually been a bit under the weather during his last visit, but the veterinarian didn't have enough information to determine the problem. You now have new information.

Medical causes for litter box mishaps include any illness that causes pain, increases urine production or impairs a cat mentally or physically. Any pain associated with the box (kidney stones, inflammation, or tumors, as well as arthritis, or spinal cord pain) can cause a cat to blame the box itself.

When older kitties begin housesoiling, it's often caused by a medical condition rather than a behavioral problem. Diseases of aging kitties, such as hyperthyroidism, kidney disease and diabetes, all cause increased thirst, which leads to increased urination. A litter box tended only once a day quickly turns into a disgusting mud hole.

Cat owners and veterinarians often mistake symptoms of vision loss, arthritis, hypertension, hyperthyroidism, deafness, or brain tumors for "normal aging changes," meaning many treatable conditions go untreated. Senior cats may also experience cognitive dysfunction that makes it difficult to simply find the box. As soon as you notice uncharacteristic behavior, take your cat to the vet. (I cover senior health issues and the litter box in Chapter 12: Senior Moments.)

Your vet will want to examine your kitty's bodily fluids, the same way a mechanic checks out a car's fluids to conclude you have a radiator problem. Instead of reading a crystal ball, your vet may just read the struvite crystals he finds in Fluffy's pee. But just because nothing shows up during your first visit doesn't mean the cat is OK. Try the treatment your vet recommends, and if the problem persists, check again. Only when Fluffy has been given the medical all-clear should you look into behavioral reasons.

Warning signs of illness include:
• Changes in eating habits; not eating, dropping food, sudden preference for canned food
  • Changes in activity level; either more or less than usual
  • Increased water consumption
  • Normally outgoing cat suddenly hides; normally shy cat hangs out in the open
  • Biting or other aggression

- Sudden weight loss or gain
- Shaking head or scratching ears
- Straining when using the litter box/attempting to use the box but producing no poop or pee
  - Tenderness in a particular area or body part
  - Overgrooming
  - Not grooming or decreased grooming

Here are the most common medical conditions that contribute to inappropriate elimination.

Anal Sac Disease

Anal gland disease is literally a pain in the bum. The anal glands are a pair of little scent pouches, similar to a skunk's stink glands, located at the 4 o'clock and 8 o'clock positions of your cat's rectum. These glands secrete a foul-smelling liquid that is normally emptied whenever he poops. While skunks use their glands for protection, cats and dogs use these secretions to mark territory.

From time to time these secretions become too thick for the anal glands to expel. Despite the clogged anal ducts, the glands continue to produce fluid, resulting in pressure, pain, and eventually infection. Because pooping hurts, Fluffy may become constipated.

It left untreated, the pressure eventually builds until the gland ruptures through the skin, draining nasty fluids and pus out of his rear. Sometimes a rupture can damage sphincter nerves and muscles, leading to incontinence.

Signs

As with most illnesses, you'll notice odd behaviors first. As always, the signs below could also be the work of other conditions. Take your kitty to the vet if you observe:

- Butt scooting: When anal sacs first start bothering him, Fluffy will do the butt-scooting boogie, dragging his bottom across the floor to relieve the pressure. Floor scooting can also be caused by allergies, itchy butts, intestinal or external parasites, or matted fur or poop stuck to the fur britches.
- Difficulty pooping: Constipation, straining or hesitation when he poops
- Excessive licking or biting of his butt and under the tail: Kitties often lick areas on their bodies that are painful.
  - Thinner than normal stool
  - Tail chasing

- A foul odor near his butt
- Swelling on the side of his rectum

Treatment

Unless Fluffy has suffered a rupture, the vet or vet tech should be able to manually empty your cat's impacted or infected anal sacs by gently manipulating the glands. Your cat will not appreciate the effort. Besides, it's stinky and messy.

⚠Don't stand too close to the procedure. Once, when a vet tech was expressing my cat's glands, a stream of anal fluid hit her in the face. I was certainly glad I left it to the professionals.

If the gland abscesses (becomes infected), your vet will need to anesthetize Fluffy before draining the infection. Your vet may prescribe antibiotics, pain relief drugs, and/or fiber supplements to bulk up his stool, making it easier to poop.

You can intervene in reoccurring impactions by regularly taking kitty to the vet or a groomer to have his glands expressed. Whenever Fluffy starts floor scooting, it's time to get the butt squeezed again. If Fluffy continues to have problems, your vet may have to surgically remove Fluffy's anal glands. Vets use this option as a last resort, because surgery sometimes leaves kitties unable to control their bowels.

Arthritis (and Other Joint Abnormalities and Orthopedic Injuries)

One study revealed that 90 percent of cats over 12 years suffer from degenerative joint disease, but kitties as young as 2 can develop painful mobility issues. Youngsters who have suffered orthopedic injuries may also experience joint pain. (You can read all about arthritis and joint disease in Arthritis, Mobility Issues and Orthopedic Injuries in Chapter 12.)

Constipation

Constipation isn't a specific disease; it's a descriptive word for the inability to regularly and easily empty the bowels. A constipated cat may poop infrequently (or not at all), or have a difficult or uncomfortable time going.

How often a kitty poops varies from cat to cat. Cats usually poop at least once a day, but a healthy cat can fill his litter box as many as three times a day.

Constipation is often a symptom of an underlying health problem. While it can happen to a cat of at any age, it's seen most often in middle-age and elderly cats. Research indicates that males are twice as likely to become constipated as females. Obese and inactive kitties also run a higher risk. While constipation is a common feline malady, it's not OK to ignore it.

Symptoms

Signs of constipation vary depending on the severity. Many of these symptoms are also experienced by kitties with urinary tract disorders, including obstructions. If he has any of the following symptoms and he's vomiting, go immediately to the vet. Contact your veterinarian if he:

- Goes more than 48 hours without making a litter box deposit
- Strains or cries out while using the litter box
- Produces smaller stool than usual or incomplete stools
- Passes hard, dry stool
- Makes repeated yet unsuccessful visits to the litter box
- Spends long periods in the litter box with little or no results
- Poops outside of the litter box
- Poop is mixed with mucous or blood
- Is dehydrated
- Lacks appetite
- Loses weight
- Is lethargic or depressed
- Is vomiting
- Has a painful abdomen
- Has a scruffy coat
- Has swelling around the anus

Causes

The possible causes of constipation range from minor to potentially fatal. They include:

- Foreign bodies such as swallowed string, bones, hairballs
- Dehydration
- Medication side effect
- Tumor
- Infection
- Pelvic abnormality
- Low-fiber diet
- Diabetes
- Arthritis (too painful to jump into the litter box)
- Pelvic or tail injuries
- Matted fur that blocks the anus

- Impacted or abscessed anal glands
- Obesity

Tails from the Trenches

Joan of Highland Village, Texas, noticed that her 3-year-old kitty, Sunny, hadn't pooped in a couple of days. The orange and white kitty wouldn't eat and simply didn't act her Sunny self. A trip to the vet uncovered the mystery. She had eaten a long piece of thread that put the brakes on Sunny's digestive tract. The string had to be surgically removed, but Sunny made a full recovery. If Joan had delayed going to the vet much longer, the kitty's prognosis wouldn't have been as bright.

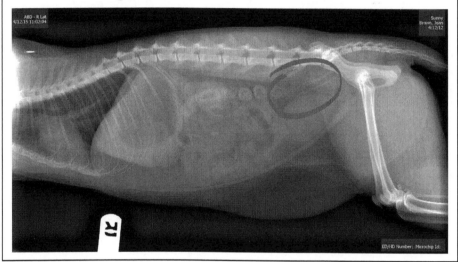

- Megacolon
- Lack of exercise
- Emotional conflict and stress
- Change of environment (hospitalization, travel or a move)
- Too fearful to approach the litter box because of another cat, dog, or even a toddler
- The box doesn't meet the cat's expectations, so he won't use it (dirty litter box, scented litter, covered box)

Diagnosis

Your vet will start by going over Fluffy's history and symptoms and invade his privacy with an anal exam, before deciding on additional tests. Don't be surprised if she takes X-rays to see if the colon is full of poop or to locate a blockage. Fluffy might have to pee in a cup to rule out bladder issues. Bloodwork, ultrasound and (in extreme cases) a colonoscopy may also be needed.

Treatment

With so many varied causes, the treatment for your cat's constipation depends on the reason he became plugged. Your vet may simply prescribe some human laxatives or stool softeners. Never give human meds without getting your vet's approval. Follow her instructions, and give the proper dosage.

Depending on the underlying cause, your vet may prescribe one or combinations of:

• **Hydration:** Your vet may inject fluids under your cat's skin.

• **Enemas:** Enemas may help loosen fecal matter. You'll want to let your vet do this dirty job, for two reasons. [WARNING!]Fleets enemas and enemas formulated for people contain sodium phosphate, which is toxic to cats. And unless Fluffy is at death's door (and if he is, he needs to see a vet), he will neither appreciate nor tolerate you shoving a plastic tube up his butt. Your effort to cleanse his colon could end up with you in the human emergency room receiving high-octane antibiotics for a cat bite. Your vet may have to anesthetize Fluffy just to gain his cooperation.

• **Stool softener, laxative:** Oral laxatives should only be used in well-hydrated cats.

• **High-fiber diet:** Your vet may switch your cat to a diet with higher fiber levels or add psyllium, canned pumpkin, wheat bran cereal or Metamucil to your cat's food.

• **Medication:** Your vet may prescribe the colonic prokinetic agent cisapride, ranitidine or nizatidine to help move material through the digestive tract.

• **Surgery to remove the bowel obstruction**

• **More exercise**

Megacolon

Caught early, an occasional bout of constipation is easily remedied. If constipation goes untreated, or after repeated episodes of constipation, the cat could eventually develop a condition called megacolon, in which the diameter of the colon to becomes exceedingly enlarged. This can result in the swelling of your cat's colon and loss of the colon's ability to move waste on its own.

Because the cat can no longer empty his colon on his own, it becomes packed with dry stool. As with constipation, you'll notice unproductive straining, but you'll also likely notice loss of appetite, lethargy, and vomiting. Without surgical removal of part of the colon, megacolon will eventually kill the cat.

Prevention of constipation

You can't completely prevent constipation, but you can help keep kitty regular by brushing him regularly, especially during shedding seasons. This keeps him from ingesting loose fur that can turn into an obstruction. Daily exercise with a feather toy will help keep things moving along. Feed a high-quality diet with adequate fiber. Provide fresh, clean water daily. If your cat tends to become dehydrated, try offering him a cat fountain.

Declawed Cats

It has been suggested that declawed cats are more likely to bite and eliminate outside of their litter box (Patronek 2001; Yeon et al. 2001) than kitties with intact paws. Such behavioral problems make it more likely for declawed cats to be euthanized.

Many cat owners believe declawing is just an extreme nail trim, but that's like saying Marie Antoinette had a short haircut. Declawing is the amputation at the first joint of the toe. The human equivalent is cutting off the tip of your finger at the first knuckle. In the case of declaw surgery, it's 10 individual amputations, all done at the same time.

While there have been few peer-reviewed studies on declawing and litter box problems, anecdotal evidence indicates that declawed cats have more problems with inappropriate elimination. According to a 2001 paper (Attitudes of owners regarding tendonectomy and onychectomy in cats) by S.C. Yeon in JVMA, the most common behavioral change seen with both procedures is inappropriate elimination. Another paper published in JAVMA by G.J. Patronek said this may be attributed to changing litter substrate for the immediate postoperative recovery period.

In "Associations Between Feline Elimination and Aggression Disorders," Dr. Karen Overall said, "Declawing coupled with premature return to gravelly kitty litter has been implicated in the development of some aversions to substrate. Cats who are reintroduced to hard litter too soon after declaw frequently develop a substrate aversion."

Imagine how painful it would feel to walk on crushed gravel after 10 toe amputations. You would probably seek out a nice, soft carpet too. Dr. Overall said, "Treatment involves environmental and behavioral modification and may require pharmacological intervention." Even after treatment, Fluffy may avoid the evil litter box, fully convinced it will hurt him again if he goes near it. Frequently vets recommend that clients fill the litter box with paper pellet litter after a declaw, but that still may not be soft enough.

"Cats most definitely can suffer pain after having their toes amputated—the appropriate description for the procedure," Robin Downing, DVM, an animal pain specialist told Dr. Marty Becker. "If post-op pain is not managed aggressively and comprehensively, the pain can become chronic," Dr. Downing continued. "Because the nerves to the toes are actually cut, the pain can become what in people is called 'neuropathic' pain. People with neuropathic pain report various sensations in the affected area of the body — they may feel tingling, burning, electrical pain, throbbing, and more."

This happens, she said, because the nerves are actually cut during the surgery, which damages them. "With nerve damage, there are changes that occur in the transmission of signals along the nerve fibers," she explained. "The damaged nerves can set up a pain syndrome that is self-perpetuating. This means that the toes can become hypersensitive, or may even develop the sensations that humans with neuropathic pain experience." In human medicine, a 2002 study lead by Pieter U. Dijkstra, PhD, found that phantom limb pain is "suffered by around 70 percent regardless the cause of amputation."

What signs might suggest to an owner or veterinarian that an already-declawed cat is suffering from a post-declaw pain syndrome? Dr. Downing said declawed cats often object to having their feet and toes touched because they experience nerve pain. Because the toes aren't inflamed, non-steroidal anti-inflammatory drugs (NSAIDs) don't work for declaw pain. Gabapentin is a different drug that "targets a receptor in the spinal cord that helps to modulate peripheral pain." Dr. Downing said, "Gabapentin is a true game-changer for these cats, restoring them to normal life. It is possible that gabapentin may have to be given for the rest of the cat's life, but every cat is different."

Diabetes, Hyperthyroidism and Kidney Disease

Cats naturally want to go to the bathroom in a safe, clean place. Some diseases of elderly cats, such as kidney disease, diabetes, or hyperthyroidism, make your cat drink more, which increases urine production, resulting in more frequent trips to the litter box. That means Fluffy cat may be filling his box more quickly than he used to. If you haven't adjusted your box cleaning schedule, Fluffy may adjust his preferred bathroom to a cleaner place. (There's a complete explanation of Hyperthyroidism and Kidney Disease/Failure in Chapter 12.)

Especially if your cat suffers from one of these diseases, scoop several times a day and give the clean litter a quick sniff. If the litter smells bad, dump the old litter, wash the box and start over.

Diabetes

Insulin is a hormone manufactured by the pancreas that regulates the cat's blood sugar (glucose). Proper levels of insulin help prevent a cat's glucose from getting too high or too low. A cat with diabetes either can't produce enough insulin, or his body can't properly use insulin. Without the correct level of insulin, the cat's body can't break down fat and protein for energy. When blood glucose rises to abnormally high levels, the sugar is filtered out by the kidneys and then eliminated in the cat's pee. Sugar in the urine causes him to pee more frequently. Because he's passing more fluids, he becomes dehydrated and needs to drink more, consequently causing him to pee even more. It's a vicious cycle.

Symptoms

Depending on the severity of the disease you may notice a variety of symptoms. Take your cat to the vet as soon as you notice any of these symptoms:

- Increased thirst
- Increased urination
- Litter box mishaps
- Dehydration
- Ravenous appetite, but still loses weight
- Walking difficulties
- Decreased activity, weakness, depression
- Vomiting
- Unkempt coat
- Enlarged liver
- Enlarged kidney
- Reoccurring infections

While diabetes can affect any kitty, it's most likely to show up in:
- Older cats
- Males
- Obese cats
- Cats with chronic pancreatitis, hyperthyroidism, Cushing's disease and /or acromegaly
- Cats on medications including megestrol acetate and steroids
- Burmese cats with bloodlines outside of North America

Diagnosing diabetes

Your vet won't be able to diagnose diabetes just from symptoms. In addition to a physical exam, she'll look at bloodwork and urinalysis to rule out infections and other underlying diseases. A single blood test showing high glucose levels doesn't mean Fluffy has diabetes. Cats are notorious for developing short-term elevated glucose levels when stressed by going to the vet or having blood drawn. That's why your vet should check the urine for glucose. Stress-elevated glucose doesn't appear in the pee as quickly as it does in blood, so high blood sugar levels should be confirmed with a urine check. Your vet will watch for persistently high glucose levels in the blood and urine.

In addition to elevated glucose levels, your vet will look for increased liver enzymes and high cholesterol levels, as well as low levels of sodium, phosphorous and potassium.

Tails from the Trenches

Susan Konecny, RN, DVM, and Medical Director for Best Friends Animal Society, had a case of a cat who suddenly began peeing everywhere, both in and outside the box. A full medical work up revealed this cat to be suffering from diabetes. Once the cat began treatment for this condition, the inappropriate urination resolved. From then on, the cat was regularly monitored in Konecny's practice.

Treatment

There's no standard treatment for feline diabetes because every cat responds to treatment differently. Some cats are easy to regulate; others take a great deal of tweaking.

Some diabetic cats can be treated with diet alone, but one-half to three-quarters will need insulin. In most cases these cats must receive twice daily insulin shots under their skin. Don't be intimidated. Diabetes needles are so fine, the cat doesn't feel them. The injection can be given by even the most needle-phobic pet owner (like me).

Most diabetic cats must have lifelong care that includes a reliable feeding schedule, because cats who take insulin injections must receive them at specific times and they should eat at shot time. Some cats can take oral medications, but these meds may cause side effects.

You'll want to work with your vet to help your pudgy puss lose weight. Never put your cat on a diet (especially a diabetic cat) without consulting with your vet. Even in a healthy cat, rapid weight loss can result in potentially deadly fatty liver disease (also called hepatic lipidosis). Because your kitty doesn't need to squeeze into an evening gown by a specific date, slow, gradual weight loss is your safest bet.

Diarrhea

Diarrhea is a catchall term for runny poop without a specific cause. It's a symptom, not a disease. Cats living in crowded homes or unsanitary conditions are most likely to develop the runs. Besides suffering with sudden and explosive urges to go, cats with diarrhea may experience painful gas and stomach cramps. They may not have time to make it to the litter box. Diarrhea can be caused by something as simple as a change in diet or as deadly as cancer.

Diarrhea may come on suddenly and resolve quickly (acute) or hang on for weeks or even months (chronic). One quick round of runny poo isn't a big deal, but if it persists for more than 48 hours, Fluffy should see his vet.

Black, dark-colored or bloody poop could indicate your cat is experiencing internal bleeding. He needs to go to the vet immediately. Also take kitty to the clinic if he starts vomiting, becomes lethargic, develops fever, strains to poop, stops eating or loses weight.

Diarrhea can be caused by any number of medical conditions, including:

- Internal parasites
- Microorganisms (giardia, coccidia)
- Sudden change in diet
- Overeating
- Food allergies
- Bacterial or viral infection
- Inflammatory bowel disease
- Kidney or liver disease
- Spoiled or contaminated food
- Contaminated water
- Colitis
- Foreign objects (rubber bands, string)
- Toxins
- Cancer
- Diseases of the digestive tract
- Hyperthyroidism
- Stressful situations
- Drinking milk
- Medications

Don't give your cats your favorite human over-the-counter diarrhea remedy unless your vet tells you to. Both Pepto-Bismol and Kaopectate contain salicylate, which is the active ingredient in aspirin—and is toxic to cats. Several years ago, the manufacturer of Kaopectate changed its formula, so the older reference books and online articles that say it is safe are no longer correct.

Your vet will examine your cat and check a poop sample for internal parasites. Sometimes protozoa or worm eggs hide from the microscope, so don't be surprised if your vet can't eyeball them. The vet may take blood, too. The treatment depends on the cause. (I'll go into more detail about many of the parasites and other causes of diarrhea later in this chapter.)

Dr. Weigner said, "Stop the diarrhea, and the kitty will make it to the box."

Inflammatory Bowel Disease

Inflammatory bowel disease (IBD), also called irritable bowel disease, is another catch-all category for a group of chronic gastrointestinal disorders that cause inflammation in the lining of the stomach and/or intestines. It's often the result of parasites, bacteria or food allergies, although many cases are idiopathic, meaning vets don't know what causes it. In some cases the inflammation is the result of an autoimmune response—the body attacking its own cells. Symptoms of IBD include diarrhea, vomiting and loss of appetite.

Vets determine the exact cause with blood work, a fecal exam, dietary trials, X-rays and sonogram. If Fluffy has an extremely frustrating case, your vet may have to anesthetize him to biopsy the intestinal lining.

Like all other syndromes, the treatment depends on the cause. It's treated through a combination of diet, corticosteriods, antibiotics and/or deworming.

Manx/Tailless Cats and Nerve Damage

The same genetic mutation that causes a tailless cat like a Manx can affect the development of a kitten's spine and spinal cord.

A cat's tail is an extension of his backbone. Rumpies, Manx born with no tail, are prone to nerve problems. The vertebrae near the Rumpy's bottom may have grown into irregular shapes, pinching the spinal nerves as the kitten matures.

If nerves to the bladder or bowels become damaged, Rumpies may experience a loss of proper nerve information transmission resulting in the inability to control the bladder and rectum. As a result, Rumpies may not be able to intentionally expel pee and poop, or close the sphincters completely. The inability to control the bladder and bowels can lead to urinary tract infections, constipation, megacolon, even rectal prolapse.

Cats who suffer tail or spinal injuries may experience the same problems.

Parasites

Parasites suck! They suck your cat's blood and steal his nutrients.

Unfortunately, the insides of a cat make a comfortable residence for a variety of unsavory organisms. Veterinary journals may list scores of the obscure feline parasites, but according to Anne Zajac, DVM, PhD, associate professor of biomedical sciences and pathobiology at Virginia/Maryland Regional College of Veterinary Medicine at Virginia Tech, the most common in the U.S. are roundworms, hookworms, coccidia, giardia, toxoplasmosis, heartworms and tapeworms.

Although usually not life-threatening, except in kittens and immune-compromised cats, internal parasites can cause diarrhea, cramping and the feeling of urgency to poop.

To diagnose most GI tract parasites, your vet will perform a fecal float. In a fecal float, the poop sample is mixed with a special solution and the parasite eggs float to the surface. Your veterinarian can view these eggs under a microscope. The presence of parasite eggs means the kitty has worms. But a negative test doesn't necessarily mean your kitty is parasite-free.

There are several reasons why the fecal exam might appear negative. There may be a low number of total worms, a prevalence of male worms, or the female parasites may not be laying eggs at that time. "No test is 100 percent," Dr. Zajac said.

Roundworms

Roundworms are the most common internal parasites in cats. Kittens become infected from the mother's milk. Cats can also become infected by eating infected prey such as mice, roaches and birds, or by using a contaminated litter box. The larvae hatch in the stomach or intestine. Here's the gross part. If they're born other places, they migrate to the liver or lungs and make their way into the intestine.

Adult roundworms produce as many as 24,000 eggs per day, which exit the body through poop and disperse in the environment, where it takes three to four weeks in the environment to become infective. The eggs can remain viable in the environment, waiting for a new animal home for months, even years. Eventually a new host licks his paws and the cycle starts over. Not surprisingly, cats in Southern states suffer infections more than those in Northern states, because of the milder climate.

Most adult cats can tolerate a roundworm infection, but kittens struggling with a heavy load may not survive. Symptoms may include: potbelly, vomiting, diarrhea, coughing and sneezing (as the worm migrates through the upper respiratory tract). Kittens may simply fail to thrive.

Humans can become infected by accidentally ingesting eggs. Ewww! (Observe reasonable hygiene. Wash your hands and don't eat cat poop.)

Roundworms can be controlled by pyrantel pamoate, or by monthly applications of a broad-spectrum heartworm preventive.

Hookworms

Hookworms also reside in the cat's small intestine. "Hookworms in cats are not as common [as roundworms]," said Michael W. Dryden, DVM, PhD, professor of veterinary parasitology at Kansas State University College of Veterinary Medicine in Manhattan, Kansas. "We don't see them in well cared for domestic cats. We do see them in ferals."

[Gross Alert]Both humans and cats become infected by ingesting the larvae, either directly or via infected prey, or through the skin. The larvae burrows through the bare skin of a cat (or human) who walks or digs in infected ground. Adult hookworms attach themselves to the lining of the small intestine with tiny hooks and start feeding just like a vampire. The hookworm life cycle takes three to four weeks, depending on how the cat became infected.

Hookworms cause anemia from blood loss in cats. As few as 100 worms can kill an adult cat. Look for pale gums, diarrhea, bloody poop and in some cases weight loss. It's diagnosed by—you guessed it—fecal float.

Once again, keep your cat inside and away from prey and contaminated soil. Your vet will either recommend deworming or regular use of monthly flea/heartworm preventives.

Coccidia

These microscopic organisms live in the cells lining the intestines. The cat ingests an egg either from grooming or eating infected prey. The eggs travel to the intestines, where the single-cell organisms mature and take up residence in the intestinal lining. They reproduce, and the new eggs pass through poop into the environment. Outside the body, the eggs must mature for a day or two before they can become infective. That's one of the reasons it's so important to scoop the box every day.

Coccidia attacks the intestines and causes diarrhea, which could cause life-threatening dehydration in kittens. Symptoms include bloody or mucous diarrhea, belly pain, dehydration, anemia, weight loss and vomiting. Again, your vet will perform a fecal float.

Vets commonly prescribe off-label daily oral doses of Albon (sulfadimethoxine) or ponzuril.

Giardia

Giardia, another species of single-cell organisms, usually reside in the lining of the small intestine. Once again, the kitty gets it by ingesting it. You know the routine.

Some cats never show symptoms, but you may notice soft stinky poop—not normally bloody—vomiting, poor body condition or weight loss. Your vet will do a fecal flotation and/or Giardia ELISA test. Because giardia sheds intermittently, it may not show up in a fecal float, so you may have to retest in order to confirm. Vets often prescribe fenbendazole (Panacur), or metronidazole (Flagyl). It's recommended that you bathe your cat after he has completed treatment, as well as sanitize the litter boxes, scoops and water bowl. The Companion Animal Parasite Council recommends treating other pets, including dogs, in the house as well. Don't forget to wash your hands after scooping.

Tails from the Trenches

As we have learned recently from the water woes in Flint, Michigan, just because your water comes from a city source, doesn't mean you can trust it.

In her 30 plus years of veterinary practice, Dr. Cynthia Rigoni had only seen two cases of giardia. However, after Tropical Storm Alison blew through Houston, she began seeing two cases a day. More recently the City of Houston's water has been plagued with cryptospirdia.

Dr. Rigoni recommends bottled drinking water for her clients and their pets, to protect them from organisms in city water.

"Don't think less of your vet if they had to send a fecal sample off to catch the giardia," she said. "I had to do a dozen in-office fecals to catch a case of giardia. We're very sorry. It's often cheaper just to send it off, rather than do it multiple times in-house."

Because in-office tests don't always find giardia, Dr. Rigoni recommends her clients get the IDEXX Feline Diarrhea Panel with DNA testing for giardia and cryptosporidium, tritricomonas, toxoplasma, salmonella, panluekopenia, feline coronavirus. She also likes the IDEXX Ova and Parasite Panel.

Toxoplasmosis

The much-feared toxoplasmosis is caused by another single-cell organism. Cats get it from eating infected prey. When the cat eats the prey, the parasite is released into the digestive tract. The organism attaches to the intestine wall and produces eggs. The cat poops the eggs into the environment. It takes one to five days, depending on environmental conditions, for the eggs to become infectious to other animals. Eventually the cat's body subdues the organisms, and they become dormant.

Humans become infected when they ingest Toxoplasma-contaminated cat poop. Bottom line: Don't Eat Cat Poop. Wash your hands. Scoop the box daily. With common sense hygiene, you'll be OK.

According to the Centers for Disease Control (CDC), "After a cat has been infected, it can release the parasite in its feces for up to *two weeks*. The parasite becomes infective *one or two days after it is passed in the feces of the cat*." The eggs can remain viable in the environment for many months and contaminate soil, water, fruits and vegetables, sandboxes, grass where animals graze for food, litter boxes, or any place where an infected cat may have pooped.

Fecal floats aren't considered accurate, because toxoplasmosis so closely resembles other organisms. Vets diagnose toxoplasmosis by the cat's history, possible symptoms and blood tests.

Keep your cat inside and away from prey. *Because toxoplasmosis takes longer than 24 hours to become infectious, it's important to scoop every day.* If you're pregnant, have someone else scoop or wear gloves when you clean the box. Wash your hands thoroughly with soap and water. Avoid handling or eating raw or undercooked meat—a more common source of toxoplasma than cat poop. Don't dig in dirt without garden gloves. Keep the kids' sandbox covered.

Treatment for your cat may include the antibiotic Clindamycin, or pyrimethamine and sulfadiazine. When you've treated all your cats (and the dog), clean the litter boxes with a diluted bleach solution (1 cup bleach to a gallon of water). Rinse it well to wash off all of the bleach. Clean up all the outside dog and cat poop, or else viable eggs can hang out in your yard for years. You can track the eggs that are on your shoes onto your floor.

Heartworms

Although heartworms aren't directly related to litter box problems, any illness can cause a cat to stray from the box. Also, I promised my friend Dr. Jim Richards I would spread the word about this deadly feline parasite.

It was once thought that only dogs suffered with heartworms, but not only do cats struggle with them, even indoor cats aren't safe. A study conducted by Tom Nelson, DVM, past president of the American Heartworm Society and medical director at Animal Medical Centers in Anniston, Alabama, found that 26 percent of apparently healthy adult cats euthanized at several Beaumont, Texas, animal shelters were infected with heartworm larvae. A North Carolina study showed a whopping 28 percent of the cats diagnosed with heartworms exclusively live inside. That makes it essential to provide heartworm and parasite protection for your indoor cats.

Cats become infected from a mosquito bite. After feeding from a heartworm-infected animal (dog, coyote, wolf), a mosquito bites a cat. Over the next few weeks, the larvae travel to the heart and pulmonary arteries, where the blood vessels begin to swell.

While rarer in cats than dogs, feline heartworm infections are more serious than in dogs. Even a single worm can cause fatal complications. Because cats show primarily respiratory symptoms, veterinarians call feline heartworm infections Heartworm Association Respiratory Disease (HARD). Symptoms mimic feline asthma: coughing, difficulty breathing, wheezing, exhaustion, vomiting and loss of appetite. A few different tests are available to diagnose heartworms in dogs and cats. Because reproductive cycles don't occur in cats, tests that are accurate for dogs are unreliable in cats. A negative antigen test doesn't mean your cat is uninfected.

Heartworm-infested cats can also get blood clots in the lungs. Symptoms can appear without even a single adult heartworm. Then again, HARD can kill a cat without even a single symptom. Heartworms at all stages, including the larval stage, can cause fatal complications.

"The disease is much more deadly in a cat than a dog," Dr. Dryden said. "More cats die of heartworms than dogs." Unfortunately, there's no cure for HARD, but your vet can relieve some of the discomfort. They then use steroids like prednisone to reduce inflammation and bronchodilators (asthma inhaler).

Vets usually put the cat on a heartworm preventive and allow the heartworms to die naturally. Virginia Tech's Dr. Zajac said, "The cat isn't the normal host. The heartworm doesn't particularly want to be inside a cat. The cat's system recognizes that the heartworm shouldn't be there. In killing the larva, it causes the worms to migrate to other locations."

Because no treatment can kill the adult or late larval stage heartworms in cats, your best chance is to use the monthly preventive. Topical monthly preventives include topical Revolution (selamectin) or Advantage Multi (imidacloprid and moxidectin), both of which kill and prevent fleas, roundworms, hookworms, and heartworm larvae. They don't affect tapeworms or amoebas.

Tapeworms

Gross as they are, tapeworms are nothing to panic about. You and your other cats can't catch them directly from Fluffy. Kitties become infected with tapeworms after swallowing fleas during normal grooming. The flea dies inside the cat's stomach and releases the tapeworm larva. It moves to the cat's small intestine and attaches to the intestinal wall.

In short order, the young tapeworm grows into a structure up to 6 inches long. At a glance that structure looks like a single body, but it's actually a head with many segments attached. Each of these segments is a separate tapeworm. As new segments form at the front, older segments break away and exit through the cat's anus as a gross, wiggly, rice-like segment containing eggs. If you missed the live performance, you may find something that looks like dried rice clinging to your cat's britches. When these sacs dry, they fall off, break open and are eaten by flea larva, to be later ingested by cats. This circle of life takes six to eight weeks.

Because it takes actually ingesting the *flea* in order to hatch the tapeworm, you and other pets won't get tapeworms directly from Fluffy, but from Fluffy's fleas.

"Tapeworms don't usually cause problem [in adult cats]," Dr. Dryden said. "They might cause digestive upset." However, a kitten with a very heavy parasite load may suffer from life-threatening diarrhea. Tapeworms give cats a bloated, potbellied look. They may experience attacks of gas, and of course there are the telltale segments making their final exits.

Contact your vet about a treatment. Dr. Dryden likes the topical Profender (emodepside and praziquantel, manufactured by Bayer Animal Health). This spot-on addresses tapeworms as well as roundworms and hookworms. Drontal (praziquantel and pyrantel pamoate, also by Bayer), which can be given by injection or orally, also eliminates tapeworms, roundworms and hookworms. Praziquantel alone, a less expensive option, kills tapeworms only.

At the same time, stop the cycle. Get rid of the fleas that cause the problem in the first place. Talk to your vet about how to control fleas in your area. [WARNING!] *Never* use a dog flea product on a cat.

With the recent advancements in parasite control, Dr. Dryden said parasite problems are completely preventable.

In old horror movies, terrified townspeople repelled vampires with garlic. Even today, people feed their cats garlic to naturally repel annoying external parasites. In his testing, Dr. Dryden has seen no evidence that garlic helps at all. In fact, feeding your cat garlic could cause life-threatening Heinz body anemia that destroys red blood cells. He said that herbal treatments, such as citrus extracts or pennyroyal, can also be toxic to pets and humans. Just because it's natural doesn't make it safe.

Using a year-round heartworm and intestinal parasite preventive decreases the risk of contracting parasites. Because several types of parasite eggs, such as roundworm and *Toxoplasma gondii*, take more than 24 hours to become infective, removing the poop right away removes the problem. Scoop daily and sanitize litter boxes and the surrounding areas.

Clean the flooring where your cat exits the litter box. You want to catch as much as you can when the cat comes out the box. The eggs get on the floor via the oils on the paws. Sanitize the litter box after completing treatment for roundworms and giardia to remove any eggs from the floor.

12   SENIOR MOMENTS

Old age ain't no place for sissies. ~ Bette Davis

Bette Davis was right. Whether you have two legs or four, growing old is tough. Not long ago, the average cat made it to only 8 to 10 years. Owners didn't have to worry about health issues of aging cats because kitties didn't survive long enough to get old. Within the past decade, though, the percentage of cats over 6 has almost doubled. Today the average lifespan of an inside cat has soared to between 14 and 18 years. Cat are even reaching deep into their 20s. According to Guinness World Records™, as of September 2016, the world's oldest living kitty was a 26-year-old longhaired tabby named Corduroy owned by Ashley Reed Okura in Sisters, Ore.

According to Cynthia Rigoni, DVM, owner of All Cats Veterinary Clinic in Houston, kitties begin to encounter senior health problems as early as 7 years. That seems way too young, but a 7-year-old cat is the equivalent of a 44-year-old person. Most cats experience at least some age-related problems by the time they reach 12.

Feline Lifestages

Life stage	Age of cat	Human equivalent
Kitten birth to 6 months	0 – 1 month	0 – 1 year
	2 – 3 months	2 – 4 years
	4 months	6 – 8 years
	6 months	10 years
Junior 7 months to 2 years	7 months	12 years
	12 months	15 years
	18 months	21 years
	2 years	24 years
Prime 3 years to 6 years	3	28
	4	32
	5	36
	6	40
Mature 7 years to 10 years	7	44
	8	48
	9	52
	10	56
Senior 11 years to 14 years	11	60
	12	64
	13	68
	14	72
Geriatric 15 years+	15	76
	16	80
	17	84
	18	88
	19	92
	20	96
	21	100
	22	104
	23	108
	24	112
	25	116

Cat to human aging chart courtesy of Arnold Plotnick
and Manhattan Cat Hospital / ManhattanCats.com

Figure 8

As humans age, we don't have the energy we once had. Our joints creak and begin to ache. We're not as flexible as we once were. We can't run as fast or as far, and the distance to the bathroom seems to have magically increased. There are a lot of similarities between elderly people and elderly kitties. Like their human counterparts, aging kitties also experience diminishing senses and mental abilities. Physical and mental decline makes everything more complicated, including answering the call of nature. In the course of aging, a model feline citizen may begin to run afoul of his toilet.

Like older people, senior cats can lose bladder tone. When the urge hits them, they may not have time to make it to the basement or all the way to the laundry room. You'll need to provide a box on each end and every floor of the house.

Behavioral changes often appear as a result of physical changes and medical conditions that occur in aging kitties. Changing behaviors such as missing the litter box, becoming more active or lazy, eating or drinking more or less, or a change in sleeping habits provide clues that Fluffy may not be feeling well. Almost any condition that causes pain or hampers mobility can change a kitty's behavior—including in the litter box.

When you notice a new behavior (such as sleeping in a different place or weight loss), it's a warning that your cat needs to see his vet. According to the American Animal Hospital Association, when kitties reach their senior years, once-a-year visits won't do the trick any longer. Close encounters of the veterinary kind should become semiannual events in order to catch and treat health problems early. After all, if your vet only sees your kitty annually, that's like you seeing your physician every seven years. While human guys may say that sounds about right, a lot can happen in that amount of time.

Senior Medical Conditions and the Litter Box

Senior kitties can suffer from so many different health issues that affect litter box loyalty. Illnesses that increase the need to pee or poop more frequently may be the underlying cause for what appears to be a behavior problem. These conditions include diabetes, hyperthyroidism, kidney disease, FLUTD, and conditions causing increased bowel action: colitis, inflammatory bowel disease and liver disease. Because most diseases are more cheaply and successfully treated in the early stages, it's important to take your golden oldie to the vet as soon as you notice something out of the ordinary.

Cats are experts at hiding illness, and elderly cats have had many years to practice. It's not uncommon for kitties to conceal symptoms of disease until the condition has become serious. Many diseases of senior cats can be controlled by simply making Fluffy more comfortable.

Stress can also cause inappropriate elimination in cats at any age, but older kitties are usually more susceptible than youngsters. Your silver citizen may be more sensitive to changes around the house than he used to be. Even something as minor as rearranging the furniture can cause a painful or cranky cat to revolt.

Take Fluffy to the vet if you notice:
- Eating or drinking more
- Eating less or not at all
- Dropping his food
- Peeing more
- Dribbling pee or peeing outside the box
- Poop looks different than usual
- Fur or skin changes
- Lumps and bumps
- Bad breath
- Bleeding gums
- Stiffness
- Panting or wheezing
- Sudden gain or loss of weight
- Tremors or shaking

Your vet may need to check Fluffy's pee and poop. Bloodwork might be necessary to determine if the cat is suffering from a geriatric illness such as hyperthyroidism or kidney disease or diabetes. A urine test can reveal a bladder or kidney infection or even diabetes. A close look at poop may expose a crop of parasites. Once they know what's making your kitty feel like what the cat dragged in, you can help get him back on track.

Feline Lower Urinary Tract Disease (FLUTD)

FLUTD describes a number of painful conditions that affect the bladder and/or urethra. Middle-aged, neutered, or fleshy felines are most at risk. Peeing outside the box is a common symptom because these conditions cause the painful urge to pee frequently. These individual conditions include:

- **Urinary Tract Infection:** This is a bacterial infection that usually affects cats over age 9.
- **Feline Idiopathic Cystitis (FIC):** This stress-related illness usually appears in cats under 10.
- **Urethral Obstruction:** A blockage in the urethra prevents a kitty from being able to pee. He may attempt to pee but pass little or no urine. This is a life-and-death emergency. Take your cat to the vet *now!*
- **Bladder stones or crystals:** Pain can cause litter box changes; sometimes these formations can block the urethra.

• **Plugs:** Mucus, crystals and other bladder debris come together to form a blob that can also block the urethra.

(Chapter 10 So Sick It's Criminal: Feline Lower Urinary Tract Disease fully explains FLUTD.)

Arthritis, Mobility Issues and Orthopedic Injuries

Osteoarthritis, a painful joint disease, is caused by the thinning of joint cartilage (the hard, smooth surface that covers the ends of the bones that form joints). This slippery surface acts as a cushion between the bones. As an animal ages and the smooth surface erodes, the body repairs it. The new surfaces grow rougher and more irregular with each repair. Once the cushion is destroyed, each step or jump causes painful grinding of the bones. (Although joint inflammation usually comes from wear and tear over time, it can also be caused by injury, infection or autoimmune disease.)

Your Golden Oldie may appear to move around the house without trouble, but achy joints may make jumping into the litter box painful. If the litter box has high sides or you've placed the box in the basement or on the top floor of the house, simply getting to the box may not be worth the effort. When Fluffy's joints start creaking like a rusty hinge, he may have no choice but to relieve himself elsewhere.

Before you say your senior kitty doesn't have arthritis, X-rays taken during a study by Elizabeth M. Hardie, DVM, PhD, revealed that a staggering 90 percent of cats over 12 suffered from degenerative joint disease. Eight- or 9-year-olds commonly suffer from painful joints, but even cats as young as 2 can develop the condition. Youngsters who have suffered orthopedic injuries may also have joint pain.

Arthritis is a progressive disease that worsens as kitties age. It can't be cured, but it can be managed. Arthritis progresses so slowly that you might assume stiffness and lack of activity are normal signs of aging.

Cats most at risk of developing arthritis are:
• Middle-aged and older cats
• Overweight cats
• Cats with congenital joint abnormalities such as hip dysplasia
• Cats who have suffered joint injuries
• Possibly declawed cats

Diagnosing arthritis

Arthritis is difficult to pinpoint in cats, so veterinary researchers fear it is vastly under-diagnosed. X-rays are helpful in revealing misshapen joints, but not always. It doesn't show up in bloodwork, and there are few definitive symptoms. Signs of arthritis pain are varied, subtle, and difficult to spot. Because cats don't advertise their pain, they certainly aren't going to show weakness in a scary vet's office, where they are likely to be eaten by ravenous vet techs.

Once again, changes in behavior are your key to how your cat is really feeling. He may stop sleeping with you because it hurts too much to jump on the bed. He may stop using the litter box for the same reason. Here's a rather lengthy list of behavior changes associated with arthritis pain (as well as with many other medical conditions):

- Litter box avoidance
- Unkempt coat, not grooming the lower part of his body
- Avoids contact with favorite family members or pet companions
- Retreats to quiet areas of the house for long periods
- Repeatedly licking or biting at his painful joints
- Joint swelling
- Muscle twitches
- Rapid, shallow breathing
- Reluctance to jump, especially to jump down
- Stiffness after active play
- Less active; no longer interested in chasing feather toys
- Sleeps more than usual
- Anxiousness or restlessness
- Difficulty finding a comfortable position; lies down and then gets up
- Trouble getting up, lying down, walking, jumping up onto favorite spots or climbing stairs
- Stops sleeping in his favorite place, especially if he has to jump up to reach it
- Vocalizes, bites or scratches when handled or touched
- Decreased appetite; weight loss
- Muscles look like they're wasting away
- Makes a grinding sound when he moves a joint
- Lameness; favoring a specific limb, limping, stiffness (a later-stage symptom)

Obesity and Weight Management

Humans often equate food with love—lots of food equals lots of love. So we leave out enough kibble to feed a Siberian tiger, creating an environment perfect for puffiness.

Figure 9 - It's easy to visualize each excess pound when you look at a pound of margarine. Photo by Weems S. Hutto.

Let's do a little Cat Math. If Fluffy's ideal weight is 10 pounds, that means the joints in his legs, shoulders and hips are rated to support 2.5 pounds per leg. When Fluffy weighs 13 pounds, those joints are supporting 3.25 pounds each; that's 30 percent more weight than the joints are designed for.

At the 2012 Greenies Feline Influencer Summit in Franklin, Tennessee, Margie Scherk, DVM, ABVP, said only 10 cat food pieces per day more than your cat's body needs can pack on 1 pound of fat in one year! That's 10 percent of a 10-pound tabby's weight. If that extra pound or three doesn't sound like much, imagine three 1-pound boxes of margarine. That's how much extra weight Fluffy is carrying around. The additional weight will eventually take its toll on his joints.

If that's not bad enough, fat cells themselves secrete hormones that contribute to the development of pain. Controlling your cat's diet and encouraging regular activity are the best ways to maintain his body weight.

Your vet can help you design a gradual weight loss program. No crash diets! Rapid weight loss can potentially cause fatal fatty liver disease (hepatic lipidosis).

Tails from the Trenches

When Shady went to her new home five years ago, she was a pudgy girl. The former owner had declawed her. Eventually Shady swelled to a staggering 22 pounds. The adopter returned Shady to the Dallas rescue group four years later because the other cats were bullying her. You think? Poor kitty could only walk and sit—nothing else. Shady got to participate in a Hill's blogger's challenge. Eating ❀Hill's® Prescription Diet® Metabolic Feline canned and dry food and treats, she lost 6 pounds in five months. That is a safe weight loss schedule for a cat. Shady can now jump on the bed and climb the stairs.

Other ways you can help your cat shed some fat include:
- **Rationing the amount of food given daily**
- **Interactive play with your cat provides exercise.** Experiment with different types of toys to find out which ones he prefers. [WARNING!] Don't over-exercise elderly or fat cats. Start your older or fat cat with mild exercise and gradually increase. No jumping as it's tough on aging or overstressed joints.
- **Food puzzles require your cat to work for food**

(You can get plenty of ideas for interesting ways to feed and play with your cat in Chapter 13 Environmental Enrichment: Just What the Doctor Ordered.)

Medical management of arthritis

Although arthritic cats don't have as many pain relief options as humans or even dogs, your old guy doesn't need to suffer. Reducing joint inflammation and managing pain are the cornerstones of providing your arthritic cat a good quality of life. Your vet can prescribe steroidal and nonsteroidal anti-inflammatories and nutraceuticals to help with those aches and pains. Corticosteroids reduce inflammation, but can only be used for short periods because of risk of developing diabetes.

Some of the pain relief drugs for feline arthritis include:
- polysulfated glycosaminoglycan (Adequan®), an injectable medication that is quite effective for some cats
  - buprenorphine
  - Fentanyl®
  - gabapentin
  - meloxicam (Metacam®)
  - tramadol

Other options include:
- ❀Tobin Farms Red Deer Antler Velvet can make walking feel less like being drawn and quartered and more like the old Fluffy. (Chinese studies also show it benefits older kidneys)
- Glucosamine, chondroitin and MSM (methylsulfonylmethane also known as DMSO).
- Nutramax Cosequin for Cats
- ❀Missing Link (Designing Health Missing LinkProducts.com; 800-774-7387)
- Alternative therapies include acupuncture, hydrotherapy, laser therapy, and massage

[WARNING!] Don't give Fluffy human over-the-counter medications without approval from your vet. Because of their unique physiology, human and even dog pain meds can kill your cat. "Cats are especially sensitive to many human pain relief medications," said Dr. Ahna Brutlag, associate director of veterinary services for Pet Poison Helpline. She said the analgesics below should *never* be given to cats.
- Acetaminophen (Tylenol, etc.)
- Ibuprofen (Advil, Midol, Motrin IB, etc.)
- Naproxen (Aleve, etc.)

If you suspect your cat may have ingested any toxic substance, call the 24/7 Pet Poison Helpline® animal poison control center (855-764-7661). This is not a free call. There is a $49 per incident fee.

Arthritis pain and the litter box

If Fluffy has celebrated his eighth birthday, it's time to set up more litter boxes around the house. No more steps. You don't make your 90-year-old granny hike downstairs to relieve herself, then struggle back up Mt. Everest to rejoin the family. Why should you expect an elderly cat to?

If a staircase stands between Fluffy and his relief station, add more boxes in easy-to-reach locations: at least one on each floor of the house, a couple on his favorite floor, and one in the room where Fluffy spends most of his time. In a sprawling home, set out several boxes so he doesn't have to go on an odyssey to empty his bladder.

Low-sided boxes

Just as elderly humans benefit from minor bathroom modifications (higher toilet seats and handrails next to the commode), older cats benefit from litter box changes. The sides of commercial boxes are too high for an arthritic cat to climb in and out. Fluffy needs large facilities with a low entrance so he doesn't have to pole vault into the box.

Arthritic cats may also experience pain while squatting to pee, causing aim accuracy issues. Standing pee-ers may inadvertently spray over the top of the box. Fluffy gets points for going in the box. It's up to you to modify the bathroom so he can use it to your satisfaction.

Replace high-sided litter boxes with boxes with a low entrance, or transform his present box or make your own. Convert a large storage box into a handicat-accessible bathroom by cutting a low entrance on one side, but leaving three high walls to protect your walls and flooring. It's easy with the tricks I share in Chapter 6 Make a More Acceptable Covered Box. ❧Nature's Miracle High-Sided Litter Box (Nature's Miracle/Spectrum Brands; Natures-Miracle.com; 800-645-5154) has a low, manageable entrance. Ramps can help your oldster access favorite sleeping places or even litter boxes.

If he still has trouble stepping into the box, try puppy pads. Fluffy need only step onto the pad. (I provide numerous options in Chapter 16 When All Else Fails.)

Figure 10 - You can make a low-entry box with just a saw and a storage container. Photo by Beth Adelman.

Have you trained your cat to use the human toilet? If so, it's time to reintroduce him to the litter box. If he's married to the toilet, provide him with steps or a ramp.

Grooming issues and mobility

As they reach their elder years, cats who were once fastidious groomers may start to look unkempt and matted. The effort to groom can be difficult for overweight cats, arthritic cats who lack their former flexibility, or cats who suffer from painful calcium deposits on the spine.

Check your kitty's anal area, especially longhaired cats. Since it's a hard area for a senior cat to reach, he might be grateful for a little help from you—although he won't act like it at the time. Remove poo clumps that may have attached themselves to the long breeches fur (you may have to do this with scissors). A quick wipe under the tail with a baby wipe after he uses the litter box will make life more comfortable for your old friend.

Also, take an occasional look at your kitty's paws. Older cats may need to have their nails clipped *more* frequently. Young cats shed the outer nail, or sheath, when they scratch the cat tree or the carpet. Senior kitties don't scratch as much, so their claws can get longer and thicker. Sometimes they get so long that the nails grow right into their toe pads. This, too, can make traveling to the box difficult.

Cognitive Dysfunction Syndrome (CDS)

CDS, sometimes called Kitty Alzheimer's or senility, can have old Fluffy asking himself, "Where did I leave my litter box?" Cognitive dysfunction may contribute to confusion, memory loss and litter box accidents.

As with elder humans, old kitties can struggle with memory lapses and lose the ability to learn. The most common CDS complaints are litter box mishaps, late-night karaoke concerts, nighttime restlessness and disorientation.

According to Dr. Vint Virga in his presentation to the 2003 Western Veterinary Conference, "Cognitive decline in older animals may manifest as any behavioral change which may be associated with a loss of memory, learning, awareness, or perception. Consequently, anxieties, aggression and elimination problems are potential manifestations of cognitive dysfunction."

Researchers don't know at exactly what age cats begin to decline mentally, but studies suggest that behavioral changes are *prevalent* in cats as young as 10 years. Other studies have shown that early signs can *appear* in cats as young as 8. By the time you notice these behavior changes, Fluffy may have been experiencing cognitive issues for some time. In one study, almost one-third of 11- to 14-year old cats exhibited at least one behavior problem related to CDS. In cats 15 years and older, that percentage leaps to more than 50 percent.

Studies of the various treatment options all agree that early treatment brings about better results, so a trip to the vet can save both you and your kitty tons of heartache. Of course, other diseases should be treated at the same time.

Signs and diagnosing CDS

Signs of cognitive dysfunction include wandering, excessive meowing, apparent disorientation, and avoiding social interaction. CDS is especially frustrating because these odd behaviors could also be caused by other diseases of aging. Because of this, your vet must first rule out pain and other age-related diseases before diagnosing cognitive dysfunction. To make it trickier, your cat might have one of these conditions *as well as* CDS. Your vet will perform bloodwork, urine tests and X-rays.

Does your cat display of these CDS behaviors?
• Misses the litter box
• Eliminates where he eats or sleeps
• Can't find his food or water bowls or litter box
• Stares into space
• Doesn't seem to recognize you, your family or other pets
• Doesn't respond to things that used to excite him: the sound of the can opener, the rattle of the food bag, his favorite toy
• Gets lost in familiar locations or stuck in corners
• Acts confused
• Wanders or paces aimlessly
• Less interested in getting attention from people and other pets
• Overly affectionate, clingy
• Not grooming
• Less interested in eating
• Acts irritable, restless or agitated, more fearful
• Decreased activity
• Urgently crying or howling, especially at night
• Nighttime wandering

Treatment

Once your vet has determined your kitty is experiencing cognitive dysfunction, the next step is to come up with a treatment plan. That will include making some environmental changes around the house and keeping your kitty on a predictable schedule.

The goal of treatment is to slow damage and death of the brain cells and

---

Tails from the Trenches

Gea, a pedigreed Turkish Van, had been a character his entire 17 years—one of those active cats who kept his humans on their toes. One day his owner found him sitting next to his flowing water fountain and crying out. At other times she found him upstairs happily eating crunchies or lounging in his favorite hangout. While he never cried while using the box, he'd squat in one box and then go to another and empty his bladder. Even after numerous trips to the clinic, his vet found nothing remarkable. The owner described his cries as "positively blood curdling." "It sounds like we're pulling his teeth without anesthesia," she said. Concerned that the cries might be pain-related, a second-opinion vet prescribed pain medication, but even on Tramadol the cries continued. After ruling out physical problems, Dr. Cythnia Rigoni, the third opinion, pronounced a diagnosis of cognitive dysfunction. After Dr. Rigoni placed Gea on the supplement ❧Senalife, the slasher movie vocalizations grew fewer and less frantic.

---

lessen symptoms. Your vet may prescribe a number of drugs or supplements to help deal with the symptoms. According to the AAFP/AFM Panel Report on Feline Senior Care, there are currently no drugs labeled to treat cats with cognitive dysfunction in the U.S. But drugs that help normalize neurotransmitter levels (such as dopamine or serotonin), and those that improve blood flow within the brain hold some promise.

• **Selegiline hydrochloride** (Anipryl®), also known as L-deprenyl: Vets prescribe it off-label for CDS cats. According to veterinary pharmacologist and behaviorist Nick Dodman: Selegiline increases the concentration of the nervous system messenger chemical dopamine, which stimulates the dopamine receptors in the brain and improves many cognitive processes. Selegiline takes at least two weeks to show improvement. This drug may interact with other medications and supplements, so tell your vet about all your cat's medications, supplements and natural remedies. Side effects are uncommon but include vomiting, diarrhea, restlessness, loss of appetite, staggering, seizure and lethargy.

Supplements

❧ **Senilife®** (Ceva Animal Health, LLC; Senilife.com) may be neuroprotective by reducing free radical production and/or increasing enzymes that destroy feed on free radicals. According to, "A Disease of Canine and Feline Brain Aging," a paper by Dr. Gary Landsberg, "the combined effect of this supplement and environmental enrichment provide the greatest benefit and, when started before the onset of behavioral signs, may extend cognitive health."

• **Activait®** studies showed significant improvement in disorientation, social interactions, and housesoiling in dogs. There haven't been clinical trials of Activait Cat®.

• **Novifit®** supplements for cognitive health contain S-denosyl-L-methionine (SAMe) tosylate. A recent clinical trial in cats showed improvement in activity, awareness and attention after 8 weeks. Best results occurred when kitties received SAMe early in the disease, rather than in more advanced cats. Talk to your vet before using with drugs that increase serotonin.

• **Apoaequorin** (Neutricks for Cats®) has been shown to improve learning and attention. It's believed that Apoaequorin provides neuroprotection.

• **Curcumin**, an antioxidant, antiamyloid, an anti-inflammatory compound found in the spices turmeric and catechin, is also thought to be helpful.

• **Cholodin®-FEL** is a dietary supplement for senior cats that contains choline, a nutrient in the vitamin B family that helps develop healthy cell membranes and maintains the nervous system. Veterinarians may prescribe Cholodin-FEL to help treat arthritis and to improve cognitive function.

CDS and litter box management

Although litter box accidents and midnight yodel-fests may make *you* want to howl, resist punishing or screaming at your cat. Your anger will only increase his anxiety and exacerbate his and your problem. Fluffy is likely wandering the house crying out, "Has anyone seen my brain?"

Here are some suggestions that may help your kitty hit the mark:

• **Don't make him go on an expedition to pee.** Leave your current boxes in place but add more convenient facilities in rooms where he hangs out. Make sure there's a box on every floor of your home.

• **Put boxes in well-lit locations or provide a night light.** He might not be able to see well.

• **Replace tall boxes with easy-to-enter boxes.**

• **Schedule bathroom breaks 15 minutes after he eats.** Take him to his freshly scooped litter box.

• **Try ❀Dr. Elsey's Senior Litter.** It's formulated to resist the growth of bacteria; it contains an attractant and offers a soft, comfortable texture.

• **Confine your cat to a single floor or room so he can find everything he needs.** Make a comfortable smaller territory that provides comfort and security, easy litter access, and allows him to avoid conflicts with the other cats.

• **Scoop more frequently.** Cats with kidney disease, hyperthyroidism or diabetes pee more.

• **Provide a predictable environment and schedule feeding, playtime and box maintenance at the same time every day, if possible.**

• **Combat nighttime vocalization by increasing Fluffy's daytime activity**, which should hopefully reestablish his (and your) proper sleep cycle.

• **Use friendly pheromones to help your cat feel less anxious.** ❀ Comfort Zone with Feliway is a comforting synthetic facial pheromone that comes in a pump spray bottle or plugin diffusers; or try ❀SENTRY® GOOD Behavior® Lavender Chamomile Cat Calming Diffuser in areas where your cat normally hangs out. (Don't spray them right next to the cat box.) Also try ❀SENTRY® GOOD Behavior® Lavender Chamomile Cat Calming Collar.

Kidney Disease/Failure

Kidney disease is a common medical condition in older cats, but left untreated, kidney disease can lead to numerous secondary health problems.

Kidneys are essential organs. (There aren't many optional organs.) They remove waste and toxins from the blood, help manage blood pressure, produce several necessary enzymes and hormones, and help manufacture red blood cells. Loss of kidney function makes your cat drink more and consequently, pee more.

Kidney failure falls into two categories.

Chronic kidney disease (CKD)

CKD is usually found in kitties over 7. It happens gradually. It is estimated to affect between 1.6 to 20 percent of cats. Over a period of years, the kidneys' ability to filter breaks down and toxins build up in the blood. These toxins will eventually begin to damage other organs. There's no cure for CKD and kidney function loss is usually irreversible. The kidneys will continue to deteriorate as Fluffy ages.

Don't throw in Fluffy's towel just yet. With early diagnosis, you can still take steps to preserve Fluffy's remaining kidney function and his quality of life.

Advances in Kidney Diagnosis

There is good news on the diagnosis front. Until recently, blood tests couldn't give you early warning of kidney failure. Blood urea nitrogen (generally referred to as BUN) and creatinine values couldn't detect decline in kidney function until there was a 75 percent irreversible deficit.

At the end of 2015, IDEXX Laboratories started offering the symmetric dimethylarginine (SDMA) test that will detect feline and canine kidney loss months, possibly years, earlier than standard BUN/creatinine panels.

Creatinine levels are influenced by muscle mass. "Older cats lose muscle mass," Dr. Roberta Relford of IDEXX said. "So [the old test is] not very accurate." BUN can be influenced by liver disease, hydration and other factors. "The big difference is, SDMA isn't influenced by nonrenal (kidney) functions."/According to IDEXX, on average SDMA detected kidney disease with only 40 percent function loss. In some cases, the animals had suffered only 25 percent of function loss. Dr. Relford said the test should be run alongside BUN/creatinine panels and urinalysis.

IDEXX now includes the SDMA test in all routine panels sent to their labs, at no additional cost. Because the test is proprietary, only bloodwork processed in an IDEXX lab will get SDMA. Neither blood analyzed at the vet's office or blood sent to other labs will provide SDMA values.

This earlier warning allows vets to discontinue any medications that may not be kidney friendly, switch the pet to a renal diet, increase fluid intake and monitor the kidneys more carefully. Early diagnosis and treatment may slow the progression of the disease.

Chronic kidney disease treatment

Your vet may recommend supplemental hydration. Encourage your kitty to drink more water with pet drinking fountains or by adding low sodium chicken broth to his water bowl. At my house, senior kitties use ❧ Drinkwell® Pagoda Fountain (PetSafe.net; 866-738-4379) and ❧Pioneer Pet® Raindrop® Drinking Fountain (Pioneer Pet®; PioneerPet.com; 866-317-6278.) You or your vet can also give subcutaneous fluids (special solutions injected just under your cat's skin). Don't panic. If I can do it, you can do it. Your vet can teach you how. (With a prescription from your vet, you can buy lactated ringers, needles and tubing much cheaper from ❧

ValleyVet.com (800-419-9524) if purchased by the case.)

Your vet will probably recommend a special kidney diet. According to Dr. Gregory Grauer's presentation to veterinarians, "New Thoughts About Kidney Disease," "Reduction of dietary phosphorus and protein intake is the cornerstone of CKD management." Dr. Grauer also recommends phosphate binders. In Chapter 10's section about diet I talk about how to transition your kitty to a therapeutic diet.

Your vet will want to monitor Fluffy's kidney function with periodic blood work. This allows the vet to adjust treatment as needed.

Nausea, vomiting, the loss of appetite and weight decline can be combated with anti-nausea meds such as maropitant citrate or metoclopramide and antacids (famotidine and ranitidine). Appetite stimulants (cyproheptadine and mirtazapine) can pique Fluffy's waning desire to eat. If your kitty's vomiting has been controlled but he still doesn't want to eat, your vet can surgically install a gastrostomy tube that allows you to place food and water directly into the stomach.

In advanced cases, your vet may recommend a kidney transplant, but transplants are very expensive and require a specialty clinic. (If you go this route, organ donors come from animal shelters. The donor may lose a kidney, but he gets a new home. Most transplant clinics require you to adopt the donor cat.)

Urinary tract infections (UTI) are rare in healthy kitties, but are common in cats with kidney disease. In one study of CKD cats, 29 percent had UTIs, so your vet will need to check Fluffy's pee regularly and treat with antibiotics as needed.

I have seen improvement in my kidney cats' appetites using ❀Tobin Farms Red Antler Velvet (TobinFarms.com; 207-586-5151.)

Kitties seldom show symptoms in early stages of chronic kidney failure, and symptoms in the later stages are usually so subtle and nonspecific that owners don't realize there's a problem. By the time your cat shows symptoms, the kidneys have already shut down 60 to 75 percent, so when you notice something is amiss, you have no time to waste. Bottom line, go to the vet when you notice these symptoms of CKD:
- Missing the litter box
- Increased water consumption
- Increased (or decreased) litter box visits
- Larger or smaller pee clumps
- Loss of appetite
- Weight loss
- Vomiting (barfing once or twice a week is not normal)
- Diarrhea or constipation

- Bloody or cloudy pee
- Bladder or kidney infections
- Unkempt coat
- Mouth ulcers, especially sores on the gums and tongue
- Breath smells like ammonia
- Brownish tongue
- Cat resting in the hunched-over position
- Doesn't want to move or be held
- Listlessness

Acute renal failure (ARF)

ARF, which occurs suddenly over days or weeks, has severe symptoms. It can happen to cats of any age. Ingesting toxins such as antifreeze, lilies, ibuprofen (Motrin®), cleaning supplies or pesticides is the most common cause of ARF, but can also be the result of an injury, dehydration, kidney infection or heart failure.

ARF is not a wait-and-see condition; it's a medical emergency. The good news is that if ARF is discovered and treated at an early stage, kidney damage can often be reversed. Vets treat ARF with intravenous fluids, medication, diet, and sometimes even dialysis. Sometimes a kidney transplant is the recommended treatment.

Contact your vet at once if you notice the sudden appearance of early symptoms of ARF:
- Increased thirst
- Increased pee volume
- Litter box avoidance

These are the later symptoms of ARF:
- Loss of appetite
- Listlessness
- Vomiting (may contain blood)
- Diarrhea (black-appearing poop contains blood)
- Breath smells like ammonia
- Seizures
- Not peeing at all

Diagnosing kidney disease

To confirm kidney disease, your vet will perform a physical exam, plus blood and urine tests. She may also want X-rays, ultrasound and in extreme cases, a kidney tissue biopsy to determine whether your cat suffers from kidney disease or something else entirely.

Hyperthyroidism

Hyperthyroidism is a common but treatable disease of middle-aged or elderly cats, and is one of the most common medical causes of litter box mishaps. It's the result of overproduction of thyroid hormones from an enlarged thyroid gland. It's often caused by a non-cancerous tumor. Because thyroid hormones affect most of the body's systems, hyperthyroidism can cause a wide range of secondary diseases and symptoms. Excessive production of thyroid hormones increases the metabolism, putting stress on the cat's heart, kidneys, nervous system, gastrointestinal tract, liver and other organs.

The thyroid gland acts as the body's thermostat, controlling how fast or slow the metabolism operates. Kitties with hyperthyroidism live with their thermostats stuck on HIGH, so their thyroid levels go up, which in turn accelerates the metabolism.

Hyperthyroidism causes increased thirst and urination. Hyperthyroid cats often have increased blood flow to their kidneys, which leads to renal washout. They can't concentrate their urine the way a healthy cat can. They may also have kidney disease that leads to increased thirst and excessive urination. So if a hyperthyroid cat is peeing more, you need to tend the box more frequently to keep him happy about going to the litter box.

Left untreated, hyperthyroidism can cause the blood pressure to soar (hypertension), as well as trigger heart, liver and kidney disease, blindness and eventually death.

Symptoms

Hyperthyroid kitties appear to have lots of energy. The kitty's metabolism accelerates to light speed. He's hungry enough to eat a hippo, but no matter how much he eats, he loses weight. He drinks more, pees more and often avoids the litter box. He grows cranky and may bite or scratch people or other pets. And he often cries out at night. Many cats who have never urine-marked may begin spraying.

Cats with hyperthyroidism display extremely varied symptoms. In the beginning the symptoms may be subtle and nonspecific, but as the disease progresses they become more pronounced. Symptoms include:

- Increased appetite
- Weight loss
- Increased thirst
- Pees more frequently, and an increased volume of urine
- Litter box avoidance
- Vomiting

- Diarrhea
- Hyperactivity (some people describe it as "acting like a kitten")
- Restlessness
- Aggression toward people or other pets
- Unkempt coat
- Rapid heartbeat (normal heart rate at home should beat 150 to 160 times a minute; at the vet's office between 225 to 230 beats per minute.)
- Increased respiration rate
- Vocalizing, especially nighttime yowling/restlessness/confusion/ behavior changes
- Dilated pupils

Diagnosing hyperthyroidism

Your veterinarian will give your cat a thorough physical exam, paying close attention to the upper front of the throat where the thyroid is located. A normal thyroid gland is so small it shouldn't be detectable when your vet palpates the throat. If the gland is enlarged enough, your vet may be able to feel it. The cat's heart rate and blood pressure should also be checked.

Your vet should run a full blood panel, including a T4 to determine the thyroid hormone level. Some cats with hyperthyroidism will have normal T4 levels. If your cat's bloodwork appears to be normal but your vet still suspects hyperthyroidism, she may recommend additional tests. Because hyperthyroidism potentially can affect so many organs, cats should be checked for other diseases, including heart disease, high blood pressure and kidney disease.

Treating hyperthyroid cats

There are now four treatment options available for cats suffering from hyperthyroidism: medication, surgery, radioactive iodine therapy, or a new specially formulated diet. As with any treatment, there are pros and cons associated with all of them. Which treatment you choose depends on the health of your wallet, your ability to medicate your cat, your lifestyle and your cat's secondary diseases.

"Hyperthyroidism is very treatable with either medication or radioactive iodine therapy, and has a good prognosis if caught early," Dr. Drew said.

Unfortunately, in a no-win scenario, often after successful treatment for hyperthyroidism, cats may develop acute kidney failure because the drop in blood pressure reduces kidney efficiency.

Medication

Methimazole (Tapazole and Felimazole) is probably the most common choice for treatment. It interferes with the thyroid gland's ability to produce thyroid hormones. Although methimazole is effective at controlling the overproduction of thyroid hormone, it's not a cure and it doesn't address the problem of a benign tumor growing on the thyroid gland. The upside is that it's relatively inexpensive. With a prescription you can get 100 tablets from DrsFosterSmith.com for about $19.

The cat will need to continue taking methimazole once or twice a day for the rest of his life. Your vet will periodically check the thyroid levels in Fluffy's blood to make sure he's getting the correct dosage, to monitor kidney function and to watch for potential side effects. Methimazole usually comes in pill form, but if your cat is difficult to medicate, it can be compounded into a transdermal cream that you massage into the inside of your cat's ear. Wear surgical gloves whenever you apply the medication so you don't absorb the drug.

Common side effects of methimazole include anorexia, nausea, vomiting, anemia, severely itchy facial skin, fever, and lethargy. Less common but more severe reactions — potentially deadly — include liver dysfunction, bone marrow disease, and bleeding problems. You will want to monitor your kitty to make sure he's eating. ALL drugs have side effects including sterile water for injection.

Once Fluffy's thyroid levels have returned to normal, your vet may discover hidden cardiac or kidney disease. That's another good reason for close veterinary monitoring.

Carbimazole is a newer drug that is rarely used and not readily available in the United States.

Tails from the Trenches

Herman, a 16-year-old Turkish Van, had peed only a few inches from the litter box for two years. He frequently vocalized and developed the bad habit of biting the hand that fed him. Urinalysis showed nothing, and even standard bloodwork appeared normal. Despite the normal report, his owner suspected that Herman's problems were medically related, and insisted on a T4 test for hyperthyroidism. Herman's results were high normal. They treated him with methimazole and his symptoms (including peeing outside the box) went away.

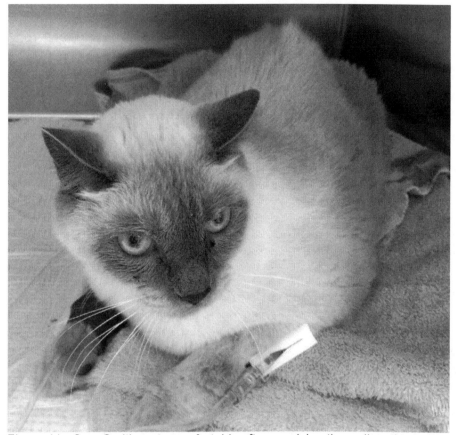

Figure 11 - Sam Smith rests comfortably after receiving the radioactive iodine that cured her hyperthyroidism. Photo courtesy of Candi Smith.

Radioactive iodine

Radioactive iodine is the treatment of choice for cats with hyperthyroidism. The downsides are it's pricey ($1,000+), a cat under treatment must remain hospitalized for three to seven days to allow radiation levels to drop—and you won't be allowed to visit your cat until he stops glowing.

This treatment uses an injection of radioactive iodine under the skin to selectively destroy the diseased thyroid tissue. It doesn't damage the surrounding healthy tissue. Most cats show normal thyroid levels within two weeks of treatment.

The positives are, it is a cure, and has a 95 percent success rate. It has no serious side effects and doesn't require anesthesia. Radioactive iodine kills the tumor and the cat should have no more problems and no further need for methimazole.

Because only specialized facilities provide this procedure, you may have to travel to the closest clinic. In rare cases, cats must take a thyroid supplementation drug after treatment.

Surgery

A thyroidectomy is surgery to remove the diseased thyroid gland. It generally has a successful track record for curing hyperthyroidism in cats. But it runs a higher risk of complications than other treatments. As with any surgery, there are anesthesia risks, which may be complicated by your kitty's age and secondary heart or kidney disease. There is also the risk that the parathyroid gland could be damaged or accidentally removed during the procedure. The parathyroid gland, which lies near the thyroid, is critical in maintaining blood calcium levels. Losing it could cause serious complications, even death.

Diet

The newest weapon in thyroid treatment arsenal is an iodine-restricted diet, Hill's y/d. As with other treatments, there are pros and cons. The diet is expensive. A 4-pound bag runs around $30 at PetSmart with a prescription. The cat cannot be fed other foods or treats while eating this food. In a multicat home, other cats cannot be allowed to eat y/d. It is not a cure.

Your vet will regularly monitor your cat's overall health and blood levels while Fluffy's eating y/d. If the y/d doesn't control the cat's thyroid hormone levels, you and your vet will have to explore other treatment options.

13   ENVIRONMENTAL ENRICHMENT: JUST WHAT
THE DOCTOR ORDERED

Life is either a daring adventure or nothing at all. ~Helen Keller

You are a great cat parent. You provide your kitty with everything he needs: food, water, a litter box, a scratching post and toys. But you may not deliver these resources in a way that makes sense for your cat.

Imagine serving a life sentence trapped in your home with all your meals provided, but no comfortable furniture, no computer, television, DVD player, nothing to read, not even a crossword puzzle. Before long, you'd climb the walls.

As extreme as it sounds, this resembles the lifestyle of many inside kitties. Unlike outdoor cats, indoor kitties don't have mice to chase or other interesting diversions.

A free-roaming cat sleeps 70 percent of his day, but when he's awake, he's working. He kills and eats between five and 10 mice a day, but not every hunt scores. Fluffy misses 15 meals for every one successful hunt. That's a lot of strategizing, running, climbing trees, hiding in small crannies waiting for prey and pouncing when a mouse appears.

Compare that to an inside cat's lackluster environment. He eats whenever he wants, but that's not a natural behavior. Boredom and a sluggish lifestyle cause stress, which contributes to litter box mishaps, spaying, hyperactivity, destructive scratching, chewing, excessive grooming, compulsive disorders and aggression.

Normal Feline Behavior

Little Fluffy on your couch evolved from the African wildcat (*Felis lybica*), a small predator who is also prey for larger predators. Today's cats still cling to many of the same quirky behaviors that kept their ancestors alive 10,000 years ago.

Activities people interpret as weird or silly are often normal actions of a free-roaming cat in the wild. Normal behaviors include:
- Eating and drinking
- Going to the bathroom
- Exploring
- Hunting (predatory play)
- Resting
- Scratching
- Sleeping
- Climbing
- Marking territory (facial marking, marking with the claws and, unfortunately, spraying)

When you provide an enriching environment, you mimic the opportunities your cat would enjoy outside. I'm not suggesting you plant red oaks and release white mice in your living room. But with a little imagination, you can convert Fluffy's life sentence into an active, challenging existence with the same freedom to express normal cat behaviors as his outdoor counterpart. You can imitate outside with clean litter boxes, elevated lounging places, hidey holes, stable scratching posts, food puzzles, cat grass and interactive toys that mimic prey that allow him to "hunt" for food.

Divert Fluffy's energy in a useful way," Dr. Dodman said. "A tired cat is a good cat." As with humans, only 20 minutes of active play is all it takes.

Think 3-D

An outside cat lives in three dimensions, climbing trees and catching some zzzzzs in the crooks of branches; it's in his genes. Kitties feel safer in an elevated position. The tree offers protection from predators, allows an excellent vantage point to spot prey, and permits him to monitor other cats entering and exiting his territory.

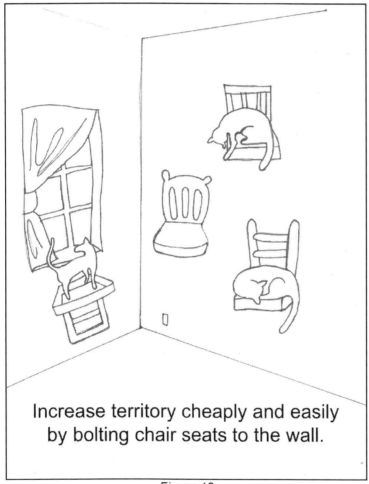

Increase territory cheaply and easily by bolting chair seats to the wall.

Figure 12

Your housecat may not have wolves stalking him, but he may have genuine concerns about both the terrier and the toddler. The more cats you have, the more lofty resting places they need to avoid conflict. To restore Fluffy's perception of safety, get him a sturdy cat tree or create an arboreal facsimile. He doesn't need a thousand-dollar carpeted cat structure. Provide a high spot by clearing best-sellers and knickknacks from bookshelves and laying out an old towel. If you have marginal handy skills, you can build a sturdy 6-foot cat tree for under $100. Free plans for Art's Scratching Post are available at my website DustyCatWriter.com. You can even buy cheap dresser or nightstand drawers at a garage sale and turn them into an elevated kitty retreat. (Don't forget to reinforce the bottom.) The Rainbolt Test Kitties love their wall-mounted ❈SmartCat® Sky Climbers (Pioneer Pet; PioneerPet.com; 866-317-6278). You can buy and install them one at a time.

Hidey Holes

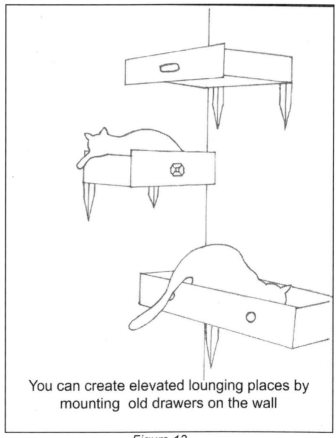

You can create elevated lounging places by
mounting old drawers on the wall

Figure 13

Cats love to hide. Confined places are the next best thing to having eyes in the back of the head. Nothing can sneak up behind them, and cozy hiding spots conserve body heat.

Several companies offer cat tunnels for curious cats to play, hide; and nap in. ❀Neko Pawdz (Nekochan ENTERPRISES, Inc. NekoFlies.com; 866-699-6356) is a fabulous tunnel system that zips into numerous configurations. Like the cat trees, a kitty hiding place needn't cost a paw and a tail. A cardboard box or a good old-fashioned paper bag (with handles removed), enclosed beds or wicker baskets can simulate a burrow where kitty can get a little privacy.

Be Your Cat's Hunting Companion and Personal Trainer

Dr. Marci L. Koski, a certified feline behavior consultant and training professional, said (after medical issues are addressed) playing with your cat and giving him opportunities to act like a predator greatly reduces inappropriate elimination.

Feline play is all about hunting. As ambush hunters, cats use their acute senses of smell, vision, and hearing to locate prey. Your indoor kitty craves these interactive experiences, and his toys should make him feel like he's stalking, chasing and dispatching prey. I know Fluffy has plenty of toys, and many of them have collected thick layers of dust and cat hair. The most intriguing toys mimic fleeing prey. That means those mouse and bird substitutes require a person to make them move realistically.

Individual cats have specific prey preferences. Some may enjoy the challenge of leaping for birds or bugs, while others may prefer to chase earthbound creatures such as mice or lizards. Identifying your cat's preferred prey allows you to provide toys and play styles your cat will actually enjoy.

Because kitties naturally hunt at dusk and dawn, these are good times to bring out the tease toys. Cats are sprinters, not marathon runners. They only need five to 10 minutes of chasing and pouncing once or twice a day.

Don't keep the toy in motion all the time; make the toy behave like prey. A mouse will run a few feet and stop, look around and then run again. Any time you play a hunting game, give Fluffy plenty of opportunities to grab the prey, hold it and bite it.

How vigorous you play with your kitty depends on his age and activity level. When he starts to pant or lie down, it's time to stop. Never encourage an older or obese cat to jump. It's painful, and bad for the joints. Run the toys along the floor slowly. Every successful hunt ends with a meal, so immediately after every play session, serve his dinner.

Fluffy will begin look forward to playtime and remind you when you overlook it.

Laser pointers are another feline favorite. Personally, I'm not crazy about them for several reasons. In the wrong hands, a laser pointer could cause eye damage. Although cats can become obsessed with a laser pointer, they aren't nearly as satisfying as other toys where they feel the prey in their claws and mouth. There's no way for the cat to win. If you do use a pointer, always begin and end the session by letting the light emerge from a power outlet. At the end of the game the red dot returns to the plug. During the game, have the dot stop on some soft toys that Fluffy can bite. Hide treats at the end of the game to allow Fluffy to eat his prey.

Almost anything can mimic scampering prey. Play Cat Kibble Hockey by sliding or tossing dry food across a hard floor one piece at a time. Kitties love to chase ribbons, pheasant or peacock feathers, or feathers dangling from wands. Peacock feathers are especially great for timid cats because it moves more sluggishly than other feathers. [WARNING!] Ribbons and toys on strings may appeal to the predator in your cat, but these toys are only safe under human supervision. If your cat manages to get his paws on unauthorized string, he's at risk of strangulation or life-threatening intestinal blockages. For safety sake, when playtime is over put string toys away where Fluffy can't reach them. I promise you, he will try.

Variety may be the spice of life, but it's also the spice of fun. Rotate toys so they are always new and exciting. Hide toys around your home so your kitty can discover them on his own.

Never let Fluffy stalk or hunt human body parts. It's not okay to tackle fingers, hands or feet. That creates hard-to-break habits.

Some of the Rainbolt Test Kitties favorite prey analogues include:

• Bird: ❀Go-Cat™ Da Bird™ This interactive birdlike toy on a string is the Rainbolt Test Kitties' all-time favorite toy because when the feather lure moves through the air, it sounds like beating wings.

• ❀Vee Enterprises PURRfect CrinkleBouncer, PURRfect Wispy Close-Up Toy

   • Reptile: ❀Cat Charmer
   • Insect: ❀Neko Birbug and ❀Cat Dancer®
   • Mouse or on-the-floor toys

Toys for older or fat cats:

• Bird: ❀Vee Enterprises PURRfect™ Go Fur It Cat Toy and ❀Go-Cat™ Cat Catcher

Solo Toys and Activities

Even more important is giving Fluffy something to do when you're away from the house. Set out interesting toys your cat can enjoy on his own, like crinkly balls and furry mice.

Toys that cats love even when you're not around:

❀Bergan® Star Chaser® with Twinkle Ball™ or ❀ Bergan® Turbo Scratcher® for Cats. (Coastal® Pet Products; CoastalPet.com; 800-321-0248) My guys can play with this trackball for hours.

❀PetSafe® The Cheese (PetSafe.net; 866-738-4379) has a feature called PLAY. While you're away, it can turn on and off twice during a six hour period.

❀Our Pets Batting Practice. (The Our Pets® Company; OurPets.com; 800-565-2695) This toy hangs off the top of a door, and squeaks electronically whenever a kitty bats or bumps against it.

You don't have to spend a fortune on cat toys. You can entice Fluffy to play with aluminum foil balls, a sock filled with catnip and knotted, plastic milk jug rings, ping pong balls and even paper scrunched into a ball.

Natural Eating Opportunities

Living in the wild is also about mental challenge. There's not much challenge to walking up to the food bowl and opening your mouth.

Natural feeding behaviors include: strategizing, locating prey, capturing, playing with, killing, and eating prey. Veterinary behaviorist Dr. Margie Scherk said that wild kitties are designed to hunt and eat eight to 10 mice a day. Not surprisingly cats prefer to eat many small, evenly sized meals over 24 hours rather than two large meals every day.

When you're home, you can get the toy out and play a quick hunting game before feeding him. While you're away, you can make meals more interesting by inventing food challenges.

Treasure hunts

"Hiding treats and toys around the house stimulates the 'seeking' part of the brain that is especially pleasurable," certified feline behavior consultant Dr. Marci L. Koski said.

According to Dr. Scherk, 10 to 15 pieces of kibble equal the caloric content of the average mouse. Place 10 kibbles each on several sheets of foil and hide them in the room where Fluffy hangs out.

"It's like an Easter egg hunt (or a scavenger hunt) every day," Dr. Koski said. "Remember how much fun that was?"

Once he's used to treasure hunts, hide the booty in multiple locations throughout the house: under chairs (not too far under), on bookcases, etc. Fluffy will have to sniff out his food as if capturing prey. If your cat eats wet food, you can place small frozen balls of cat food on sheets of foil around the house.

Of course, this gets more complicated (and possibly impossible) if you have multiple cats or dogs. Each cat should have his own dining area, not side by side. (That makes it way too easy for dominant cats to guard all the bowls at once.)

Food puzzles

Food puzzles encourage kitties to forage rather than gorge. You may need to show your cat how to work the puzzle. If it's adjustable, start out on the "easy" setting. Once you're confident he knows how to feed himself, gradually make it more challenging. Eventually the puzzle can replace his food bowl.

I set up the SmartCat Peek-A-Prize Toy Box (Pioneer Pet PioneerPet.com; 866-317-6278) and Catit Senses 2.0 Digger (Rolf C. Hagen; Catit.com; 800-724-2436) puzzles and the Test Kitties actually passed up full bowls of cat food to solve the puzzles. Dr. Buffington said this preference to work for food is called *contra-grazing*.

Kitties pass up full feed bowls to forage from:

• The Rainbolt Test Kitties' favorite food puzzle is the ❧SmartCat™ Peek-A-Prize Toy Box or the smaller ❧SmartCat™ Peek-and-Play (Pioneerpet.com). These pressed wood boxes have rows of round openings just large enough for a cat ball. To make these boxes into intriguing food puzzles, stuff it full of your cat's favorite balls/toys. Use different types and textures of balls and small toys (catnip, sparkle, glowing, blinking, fuzzy, fur mice, fake fur, etc.) Mix his kibble in among the playthings and make Fluffy dig around for his toys and food.

❧ PetSafe® Egg-Cersizer™ Cat Toy (PetSafe.net)

❧ Catit Senses 2.0 Digger (Rolf C. Hagen CatIt.com; 800-225-2700)

• Bird: Toilet paper roll puzzle. Make a puzzle from an empty toilet paper tube. Seal the end of the roll with duct tape and punch holes larger than your cat's kibble. When you first introduce the puzzle, make the holes large to easily dislodge dry food. Next time you have an available roll, make the holes a little more challenging.

❧ PetSafe® Cat Fishbowl (a little more difficult than Egg-Cersizer)

Tails from the Trenches

Dash, a flamepoint Siamese-mix, had a reputation for being aggressive. Dr. Marci Koski taught his owner, David, to clicker train his beloved but intolerant kitty. David played with Dash twice a day and began hiding treats around the house. Within a month Dash transformed into a friendly, outgoing cat who looked forward to his twice daily play times. He got the mental stimulation he needed as a predator. He began associating humans with a more exciting life.

Water

Successful environmental enrichment also provides your cat with water from an appealing source.

"We do know that cats have different preferences for the manner in which water is offered," said Linda Ross, Associate Dean for Clinical Programs and Hospital Director as well as Associate Professor of Small Animal Medicine at the Department of Clinical Veterinary Sciences at Tufts University School of Veterinary Medicine.

One size, or one cat waterer, does not suit all. One of my Turkish Vans stuck his foot in the water bowl and licked the water off his paw. You may have to experiment to see what type of bowls or water source your kitty prefers. Some like stainless steel; others opt for ceramic or glass. Because plastic bowls are hard to sterilize, they harbor bacteria and have been associated with feline acne.

Cats are sensitive to the temperature, taste, freshness, aeration and movement of water. That's why cats and dogs often sneak drinks from the toilet. Commode water is usually cooler than H2O sitting in a plastic bowl—and it's refreshed every time you flush. Likewise, ceramic or steel bowls keep the water cooler than plastic. Be sure to change the water at least once a day.

Some cats prefer to drink water running from the tap (if they can train their humans). If your cat is a spigot sipper and you don't have time to turn on the water 40 times a day, try the ❧ Oasis Thirst Quencher Dog Waterer (Kordon, LLC. Kordon.com/oasis; 800-877-7387.)

If your cat has a condition that requires additional water intake, here are a few tricks you can try.

• Keep the bowl as full as possible so kitty doesn't have to stick his face down into the dish. Some cats don't like bumping their sensitive whiskers against the sides.

• Your cat may not like the taste of the water in your area. Try filtering the water or give him bottled water.

• Put a few drops of tuna or salmon water, chicken broth or clam juice in a separate water bowl, or make catsicles out of broth and water.

• Let him drink wherever he wants, but keep his water bowl in a quiet area and well away from the litter box.

• Try tossing an ice cube in the water and see what happens, or add refrigerated water.

• Change the water at least once a day.

• Provide pet drinking fountains.

Pet fountains

Pet drinking fountains simulate running water that cats enjoy in the wild. The mini waterfall oxygenates the water, which inhibits the growth of bacteria. The sound of trickling water also attracts some cats to drink.

If you provide a pet water fountain, keep in mind that filters won't prevent algae and bacteria growth. Just three days after I set up new cat fountains, I found a slimy film growing under the waterline. Film can also form inside the pump.

As with traditional water bowls, change the water daily; don't just add water. When cleaning the fountain, open it and wash the interior. Most fountains are dishwasher safe on the top shelf, but make sure to scrub all the crannies where bacteria and algae hide. If your pump no longer works properly, some brands allow you take them apart and remove the cat hair and film from the propeller.

[WARNING!] A couple of warnings: Don't let your kitty drink from plastic and polyresin decorative fountains. They aren't safe for drinking, as chemicals can leech into the water and resin can flake off, where the kitty can ingest them. Also, they aren't designed for cleaning so they can harbor bacteria, mold and algae.

[WARNING!] Also, if your cat likes to drink from a drinking glass, make sure the mouth of it is wider than your cat's head. There have been tragic cases where the cat's face became suctioned inside the glass.

The Test Kitties' favorite drinking options include:

❧ Drinkwell® Pagoda Fountain: This stylish ceramic design is easy to clean and looks great. The tower recirculates and aerates 70 ounces of water into a ceramic bowl from two spouts. Both the unit and the pump can be opened for cleaning.

❧ Pioneer Pet® Raindrop® Ceramic Drinking Fountain: This attractive ceramic fountain would fit in any room because it resembles a decorative fountain. It's dishwasher safe, uses a replaceable charcoal filter and has 128-ounce capacity.

❧ Oasis Thirst Quencher® Dog Waterer: For people who are slaves to turning the kitchen faucet on and off, this heavy-duty waterer offers fresh water on demand. A lick of the lever releases the water directly on the cat's tongue. When not in use, the water shuts off. It requires a 2E Dishwasher aerator adapter, available at any hardware store.

As with food or litter box changes, if you want to change your cat's current water delivery outlet, leave his old water bowl in place and offer the new option nearby. Fluffy will show you which option he prefers. And remember, food and water bowls should be washed daily.

Scratching Opportunities

Scratching is another natural and necessary, but unappreciated feline behavior. Kitties communicate with other cats by leaving visible and olfactory messages on tree bark (or sofa arms)—another form of feline graffiti. Because he's marking with his paw pheromones, scratching objects discourages marking with pee.

Scratching is more than texting messages; he's also conditioning his claws, toning his muscles and getting some exercise. It's such an intense, instinctive behavior that it's impossible to stop. You can, however, channel this drive to a more acceptable target.

Fluffy loves the furniture because it's the most stable scratching surface in the house. Watch a kitty ripping into a sofa arm. You'll see he puts his entire body into it. It feels great! No matter how hard he yanks, it doesn't move. Forget the worthless little scratchers hanging from the doorknob or wobbly cheap scratching posts. If your cat avoids his designated scratcher in favor of your La-Z Boy®, he's telling you whatever you've offered him isn't close enough to a natural tree.

Number one on Fluffy's list of prerequisites is stability. When picking out a scratcher, look for a heavy post with a broad base that won't budge even when your cat gives it a full-body yank. Think of it this way: At the fitness center, when you get on equipment that wobbles, you move. Fluffy's doing the same thing. Test a potential post before you shell out money; poke the top of it with your finger. If it moves at all, rest assured, your cat won't use it. It's better to spend a little more, and keep Fluffy happy and your furniture intact. Fluffy also wants to stretch his spine. You're wasting your money on a post shorter than 30 inches tall.

Cats also have tactile preferences. They usually prefer sisal-covered scratching posts. This rough twine may feel like natural bark to him. Your kitty may favor another texture, like carpet, wood, loose-weave fabrics or cardboard. Keep trying until you find a material your cat likes. (If you buy scratchers from one of the big pet suppliers, they have a 30-day return policy. You can return an ignored scratcher or tree.)

❧The Ultimate Scratching Post is the best affordably priced (suggested retail price is $74.99) scratching post, and it's a longtime Rainbolt Test Kitty favorite. It fulfills all of the feline requirements: it's tall, stable, covered in sisal fabric. And to appeal to people, it's inexpensive (compared to cat trees), durable, portable, takes up little room, and looks nice.

If budget is an issue, try setting out a large oak log or pick up an angled cardboard scratcher. Angled scratching pads appeal to many cats, giving them a combination vertical and horizontal scratch in one. They're so inexpensive that you can scatter them throughout your home. The Test Kitties also loved ❧M.A.X. Endeavor Cat Scratcher (CatClaws.com 800-783-0977) because it has both horizontal and vertical scratching surfaces and a hidey hole.

Location

Any real estate agent knows the most important selling feature of any property is location. Placing the scratcher near a sunny window ups your chance of scratching success. So does placing it next to the shredded furniture. Repel him from the upholstery with ❧Sticky Paws® Furniture Strips (PioneerPet.com). ⚠Don't use Sticky Paws on leather. After he's using the scratching post or cardboard pad, you can move it toward your preferred location a few inches at a time.

If your cat is attracted to catnip, rub some fresh herb onto the post or pad to get his attention. Once he's claimed it, he'll keep going back to it.

Kitty Entertainment System

You can turn a boring day at home alone into a more interesting existence by providing him with his own entertainment system.

• Window perches: If your cat isn't overly reactive to outside animals, provide visual stimulation with a window perch. Set up a bird/squirrel feeder or a bird bath outside the window so Fluffy can watch his own version of reality TV. You don't have to spend a dime. Set a kitchen chair or hassock next to the window and open the curtains. (Outside entertainment might backfire if Fluffy tends to blow up at the sight or smell of neighborhood cats, dogs or wild animals wandering into his yard.)

• Purchase feeder crickets from Petco or PetSmart and let Fluffy hunt.

• Fish tanks: Be sure to put a secure cover on top of the tank to protect the fish.

• Cat videos/DVDs: You can buy DVDs specifically to entertain your cat, featuring super close-ups of birds or squirrels hovering around a feeder. Kitties have short attention spans. He may grow bored after just 10 minutes.

• Cat garden: Most cats enjoy nibbling on grass from time to time. Offering Fluffy cat grass or live catnip is a great way to stimulate his sense of smell.

Catnip Party

There's nothing like a party to get everyone in a good mood and relieve stress. Cats usually pee or spray on the outer edges of their home territory.

Figure 14 - Groucho enjoys a little whiff of catnip. Photo by Weems S. Hutto.

Have you ever seen the movie, *Animal House*? Even the Delta fraternity lowlifes didn't piss on the floor of their Party Pigsty. Like the Delta frat boys, your kitty instinctively doesn't want to relieve himself inside his home base. A catnip party, held atop a past pollution point, repurposes the Latrine Locale into the party room.

After removing all traces of pee from the floor and walls (Read Chapter 7 Crime Scene Cleanup to learn how to do it effectively), invite your little offender into the room and start the party. For a rocking soiree, offer Fluffy both fresh and dry loose catnip, and of course catnip toys. For the best response the catnip should smell very minty. The Rainbolt Test Kitties would do time to enjoy ❧Ducky World Yeowww® (DuckyWorld Products,

Inc.; DuckyWorld.com; 866-493-6999) loose catnip and catnip toys. They even have misdemeanor-size bags of catnip. You can pick up ❀Bellrock Growers (Bell Rock Growers, Inc.; BellrockGrowers.com; 888-943-2847) live catnip online and at PetSmart and Petco. Sprinkle the catnip on the floor and watch as Fluffy acts like a goof. This encourages face marking as Fluffy rubs and rolls around. Yes, you'll have to vacuum, but so what? You have to clean up after any great party.

Feline Fact or Fiction: All Cats Love Catnip

While it's true all species of cats, from the tabby to the tiger, respond to catnip, not every individual cat can enjoy it. The ability to respond to the catnip is an inherited trait; 25 to 30 percent of domestic cats genetically lack the ability to react to it. If your kitty has never been impressed by the herb, offer him honeysuckle cat toys ❀Kitty Kottage Honeysuckle Toys (KittyKottage.com; 888-527-4704) or dried lavender in a sock. Don't use lavender potpourri because it may contain essential oils that are toxic to kitties.

It would be a boring party without entertainment and refreshments. Unleash your cat's favorite tease toy, and turn it into a puss piñata. Make him run and jump to attack the lure. When the game is over, feed him. Between parties, place his food and water bowls, bed, and favorite toys in the formerly soiled area. Frequent parties will transform his toileting area to home base, making your cat less likely to pee there.

Calming pheromones

Many respected behaviorists swear by introducing Feliway® calming synthetic facial pheromones into a cat's environment to help decrease anxiety-related behaviors in cats. My little clowder has also had positive results when I plug in a Feliway diffuser where they hang out.

As I've said throughout the book, nothing works on every cat in every situation. There have been numerous studies on Feliway. Although numerous studies show Feliway is highly effective at reducing kitty stress, others conclude it's not effective. It's certainly not going to hurt.

I have also had good results from the ❀Sentry HC Good Behavior Pheromone Collar in reducing aggression in my visually challenged cat, BK.

Pheromones' effectiveness may be improved by combining them with environmental enrichment or drug therapy.

The Safe Outdoors

You can provide your cat with all the stimulation of outside living with safe, limited access. Families with more disposable income can install cat fences, enclosed porches, window enclosures, and window perches. Being able to run, play and climb trees relieves stress. It uses up excess energy that would otherwise be spent tormenting less dominant cats or destroying your home.

Build a catio or a backyard enclosure

A screened-in patio enclosure can give your cat the thrill of being outside but without the risks. This allows Fluffy to sunbathe and enjoy fresh air without the hazards normally associated with the outdoors.

Do fence me in

A cat fence isn't a cheap option, but it might be more cost-effective than replacing your carpeting every few years. Most cat fences are plastic mesh attached to a standard backyard fence via brackets. The Rainbolt Test Kitties have enjoyed the benefits of a cat fence for more than 20 years. Sixteen years ago we switched to the ❧Affordable Cat Fence (CatFence.com).

The cats can spread out in the yard, dig, enjoy the fresh air and snooze in the garden. Over 20 years in a multicat household, a couple of kitties have figured out how to escape. (If you have trees, you'll need to trim them as they grow. The trees are our fence's Achilles heel.) However, with those two exceptions, it's kept everyone safely in the yard. Your own fence must be sound. The most secure cat fence in the world won't hold a kitty if he can squeeze through holes at ground level.

If you don't already have a fence, consider the ❧Purr. . .fect Fence™ (PurrfectFence.com; 888-280-4066.) I have never personally used it, but I have interviewed numerous feral cat managers who say it is the best freestanding fence available.

Cat walks

When we think of taking a pet for a walk, we immediately think of a dog, but felines have been going on walks for thousands of years. Surviving paintings from the tombs of Egyptian Pharaohs depict the cheetahs on leashes at the hunt.

Before you rush right down to your favorite neighborhood pet supply, consider your kitty's personality and temperament. Would he enjoy a walk? Don't traumatize cats who are anxious, timid or hide at novel experiences. Walks are for cats who walk around confidently and own an investigative nature.

Don't take him outside with something unfamiliar wrapped around his body. Put a cat harness on him for a brief session while he eats. ([WARNING! Never connect the leash to the cat's breakaway collar. Make sure he's microchipped and wearing ID tags.) He's going to accept it or not. If you have to work really hard to make him accept the harness, he probably won't enjoy a cat walk. It's like parents trying to turn their 2-year-old child into a violin star. If he doesn't have an appreciation for it, all of the effort will be in vain.

14 OUTSIDE CATS AND RESTRAINING ORDERS

I found out why cats drink out of the toilet. My mother told me it's because
the water is cold in there. And I'm like: How did my mother know that?
~ Wendy Liebman

When you rescue a kitty, you probably know little or nothing about his history. You don't know whether he's ever used a litter box or if he simply pees and poops wherever he wants to. Let's assume the litter box is a brand new concept to him. You'll want to transition him from an outside cat to a box-using inside kitty.

Start the indoor process by taking Fluffy to the vet. Because intact kitties have more problems with urine marking, get him or her fixed. While you're at it, have your vet address internal (and external) parasites that can cause intestinal issues (translate to diarrhea) and update his vaccinations.

There are two schools of thought about bringing kitties inside.

1. If you had to have Fluffy fixed, you can use his/her recovery period to your advantage. When you first bring him home from the vet and he's still feeling a little out of sorts, introduce him to his personal sanctuary. Outfit a small room or bathroom with everything he'll need, including a large, open, cat-friendly litter box.

2. Some behaviorists believe transitioning cats gradually inside is the best way to go. If you currently feed Fluffy outside, set his supper just inside the door. After his meal, play with him. Introduce Fluffy to his litter box by offering it and using a toy to lure him to take a step in. Each visit, keep him inside for increasingly longer periods.

This process might go much quicker when winter approaches and temperatures begin to plunge. When it's cold outside, Fluffy might be more content to sleep by the fire.

Litter box training

The term "litter box trained cat" is something of a fallacy—certainly an exaggeration. Unlike dogs, who have to be trained to pee and poop outside, kitties instinctively go in loose material and cover their waste inside their home territory Dr. Buffington said. If you put a 4-week-old kitten in a litter box after feeding him, he'll instinctively pee and poop like a big kitty. No training necessary.

Sanctuary

Whenever you first bring home a new cat or kitten, start by confining him to a safe room so he can transition to his new life (and your home) gradually. (I give you info on introducing a new cat to your home in Chapter 9 Hurry Up in There! Potty Issues in the Multipet Home.) Place him in a small room, perhaps a bathroom, outfitted with food and water, a comfy bed and a cardboard scratching pad or cat tree, and on the opposite side of the room, a cat-friendly litter box.

This isn't a punishment. You're helping him establish this room as his territory. Because he's going to want to cover his scent, he will seek out the litter box. Pick up bath mats and rugs. The litter box must be his only option to cover his poop. Within the confines of a small room, he will naturally want to seek out loose material to hide his waste.

He's likely going to be scared, or at least confused, so offer him a hiding place like a box or paper bag (with handles removed). A cubby hole or hiding place lets him observe the activity in his environment from a place of safety.

If you're thinking about using an electronic self-scooping box, this isn't the time to introduce it. (I cover all kitties' bathroom preferences in

Chapter 6 Thinking Inside the Litter Box.) Neither will an outside cat be enthusiastic about pooping in scented or large-grained litter. Provide a big open box—the bigger the better. Remember, he has been using the Great Outdoors as a litter box.

Make the cat box filler as enticing as possible. If he doesn't catch on to the purpose of sandy, unscented cat litter, he might prefer a litter closer to what he's been using on the street.

Try filling the box with:

• Fine, unscented litter

❧ Dr. Elsey's Touch of Outdoors™ cat litter (PreciousCat.com). The good people at Dr. Elsey's have formulated a litter especially for transitioning cats or cats who long to go outside. It contains natural chemical-free prairie grasses to help bring the outdoor experience inside.

❧ Dr. Elsey's Cat Attract™ cat litter

• Topsoil from outside

• Potting soil without fertilizers or insecticides. One study showed most bags of commercial soil contain parasite eggs. Make sure your newly inside cat is on a monthly parasite preventive. Wear gloves when you handle the soil or wash your hands thoroughly after handling it.

• Sand

❧ CatSpot Litter. (CatSpotLitter.com; 844-624-3125) Has the advantage of feeling and smelling like natural dirt, most likely without the concerns of being infected with parasite eggs.

Scoop every time you visit the cat's room. Dirt and sand don't have ingredients to control odor, so change the box filler daily. As he becomes more comfortable with the box concept, you can add unscented litter to his box.

Visit new Fluffy often. Spend time with him in his sanctuary. Read to him, play with him, give him treats, and if he likes it, brush him.

"It is an unnatural thing to be kept indoors." Dr. Dodman said. "There are certain things cats give up and things the owner need [to do] to make up for the cat's lost entertainment outlet." He suggests owners need to play with their cat and exercise him. Cats need toys to stimulate their predatory tendencies; things that make him run and chase and jump.

Once he's consistently using the litter box, you can start letting him out of the sanctuary on supervised outings. Each time, keep him out for longer periods. If you notice him sniffing around, say nothing. Calmly and gently pick him up and place him in the litter box. When he goes, give him lots of praise.

When Fluffy has full run of the house, leave the litter box where it is in his former sanctuary. If you don't want a permanent litter box in that spot, place a second box in your preferred location. You can slowly move this sanctuary box closer to the permanent spot. When the two are close together, you can eliminate one.

Once he's allowed to roam free, if he has a litter box lapse, return him to the sanctuary.

He may be tempted to use your inside flower pots as a toilet. A pot with a plant makes the perfect bathroom, and it smells just like his old toilet. He won't understand why you're upset. Make your potted plants unattractive by simply adding a layer of gravel on top of the soil.

Outside Cats and the Neighbors

People with outside cats should want to be good neighbors, if for no other reason than for Fluffy's own safety. Even if your neighbor Mrs. Smith loves kitties, she'll likely explode if she grabs a handful of cat crap when she's weeding her garden. If Mrs. Smith doesn't like cats, Fluffy could become the target of poisoning or other cruelty. This is yet another reason to keep Fluffy fenced in your own yard. (Check out fencing options in The Safe Outdoors in Chapter 13.)

If Fluffy happens to be an outside stray you are feeding, and he finds your neighbor's vegetable garden irresistible (and who wouldn't love to bury his poop in freshly tilled soil?), you can discourage him by making the garden unattractive while providing a designated yet enticing toileting option. You may also want to create a specific toileting area for your own pet cats who spend time in your securely fenced yard.

Outdoor litter box

OK, it seems redundant to offer outside cats an alluring litter box, but if it keeps the cats out of your flower bed, it's worth it. The outside techniques aren't that different from the options mentioned in Chapter 15 Litter Box Rehab and Chapter 8 Cat Tagging: When Kitty Marks.) The trick is to make the litter box more appealing than the flower beds.

Pick an area not too far from the kitties' preferred toileting spot. Pour sand or ❧Precious Cat® Senior litter (Preciouscat.com) over a weed barrier cloth. Instead of throwing away my cats' used Precious Cat® Senior, when I change the boxes, I pour the old litter in a designated pooping area. The silica gel doesn't dissolve and the cats automatically seek it out. You can even make a cheap simple frame out of 2-by-6 lumber seconds or landscaping blocks. You'll have to scoop the poop, but hopefully it will keep the cats out of the vegetable garden. Here are some other options to keep kitties out of the garden:

❧ Scarecrow®: A motion-activated water sprinkler
• Ultrasonic motion-activated devices

• Spread fresh citrus peels where the cat deposits his personal fertilizer. Use a food processor or blender to chop them up and blend it with the soil

• Pepper the soil with pine cones, sticks, rocks, sharp gravel, even chopsticks to take the fun out of digging.

• Commercial cat repellants: As with inside cat repellents, you must treat the area regularly

• Chicken wire on top of the dirt makes digging uncomfortable for cats. Cut holes in the mesh to allow the plants to grow.

"Fortunately, rehab confinement isn't solitary confinement."

15   LITTER BOX REHAB

If a cat can detect no self-advantage in what it is being told to do, it says the hell with it, and if pressure is brought to bear, it will grow increasingly surly and irritable to the point where it is hopeless to continue.
~ John D. MacDonald

165

To reduce the rate of recidivism, many prisons provide education and rehabilitation programs, as well as psychiatric care to help prisoners deal with mental disorders and psychological issues. After their release, prisoners who have stuck with these rehab programs stand a better chance of succeeding and becoming productive citizens. Emulating the prison system, you need to create a litter box rehabilitation program to reduce the chance of relapse, so your cat can once again become a valued and welcome family member.

Prerequisites for Litter Box Rehab

From reading other chapters, you know the state of Fluffy's health and you've determined whether he's spraying or peeing or both. The covered litter box now resides in the local landfill, and you've replaced it with spacious, open facilities filled with desirable litter. There are enough litter boxes for all your cats and you've taken steps to protect him from other pets who harass him while he's answering nature's call. The boxes are scooped daily (or more) and the litter is changed and the box is washed as needed. Finally, your carpet has been thoroughly cleaned.

And if, after all that, Fluffy continues to anoint the carpet, it's time for your repeat offender to go into a rehabilitation program.

Temporary Boarding

If you haven't been able to make all the environmental changes (thoroughly clean the house, block rooms, assemble deterrents, set up new litter boxes, etc.) with Fluffy underfoot because he's reannointing the carpet faster than you can clean it, consider boarding him at your vet's office while you complete your honey-do list, or make the changes while he's in rehabilitation confinement.

Not So Solitary Confinement

Now, let's get this straight: He's going into rehab, he's not being punished. Confinement creates a new home base for him. Also, kitties instinctively won't eliminate where they eat or sleep. Confined within a small space, Fluffy should feel compelled to go to the bathroom *inside* the box, whereas with free run of your home he has endless space to avoid his box and still not risk contaminating his dinner bowl. When he's reliably using his litter box, you can gradually open up the house to him—under supervision.

Create a sanctuary for Fluffy in a bathroom, or another small room with no furniture. Lead Fluffy not into temptation. Remove carpets, bathmats, or other texture your kitty likes using as a toilet. If he likes fabric, don't offer a cat bed or blanket. Instead, let him lounge on a shelf, a cat tree, inside a cardboard box or a paper bag. To deter a kitty with a fondness for peeing on smooth surfaces, pour an inch of water in the tub or sink if he's in the bathroom. Put his bowls and bed opposite his litter box. Offer him a litter box cafeteria so he can show you which cat litter and litter box *he* prefers. (I explain this in Uncover Your Cat's Litter Box Preferences in Chapter 6.)

If you don't have a spare room, you can put him in a very large cat cage that has two or three lounging shelves at different heights above the floor, or a cage or crate large enough for a Great Dane or Saint Bernard. Keep the crate/cage where everyone hangs out, so he can still be part of the family.

Don't ignore him. During his confinement, he needs activities, socialization and exercise. Go into his room as often as possible and spend time with him several times a day. Cuddle with him, read to him, get his favorite toy out and play chase the bird. Give Fluffy every opportunity to succeed. Scoop his box several times a day while he's locked up. Don't expect results overnight. It will take at least two to four weeks of the same routine to develop his new habit.

When Fluffy begins to consistently use the litter box while in detention, reintroduce him to the house one room at a time. Release him on five-minute supervised excursions. With each successful visit, gradually increase the time outside his room by a few minutes. Make sure there's a litter box in whatever room he's visiting.

If you catch Fluffy sniffing around the room, calmly pick him up and gently set him down in his box. Tell him what a good boy he is. If you have a treat handy, reward him after he uses the box. (Later, check the area he was sniffing with a black light to make sure there's not a pee spot that needs cleaning.) Return him to his room when you can't keep an eye on him, to prevent unauthorized piddling.

If he sneaks an inappropriate pee, take him back to his room and shorten his next excursion.

In addition to setting up new boxes in visitation rooms, continue to make the litter box in his detention center available so that he can return to his territory to pee if he prefers.

Making Inappropriate Elimination Unpleasant

It's the nature of any animal to repeat enjoyable actions and avoid the unpleasant. If your home had one, clean fresh-smelling bathroom stocked with interesting reading material and a second cramped potty reeking of stomach-churning odors, you'd go to the pleasant facility.

I'm betting Fluffy will do the same. That's why, after thoroughly cleaning his mishaps (You can learn about that in Chapter 7 Crime Scene Cleanup,) you're going to make his litter box an enjoyable place to read a magazine, while at the same time block access to his taboo toileting area. If you can't bar Fluffy from his pee spots, make his targets so unappealing that he won't want to go near them. Place an acceptable box near the target.

As always, no strategy works on every cat. Some cats actually like peeing on textures that send others running. You'll only know through trial and error. Just as Fluffy's confinement may take three to six weeks to break a habit, to fully break the habit you'll also continue to make the area unpleasant for that period. After he begins using his boxes, gradually remove the deterrents. If he relapses, or starts sniffing around the old spot, return the deterrents.

Here are some options to keep Fluffy away from his target.

• **Close the door.** Simply prevent access.

• **Motion sensor deterrents.** ❧Ssscat® (PetSafe.net) is my favorite cat repellent device. It's a burst of compressed air activated by a motion sensor. This is the perfect deterrent because cats hate it, it works every time 24/7 and it doesn't affect pets who are not in the area. Although Ssscat is expensive, it's very effective. You can also set up an inexpensive audible motion-detecting alarm. That one will irritate everyone, guilty or not, including you.

• **Adhesives.** Cats hate the sticky feel of adhesive. Place double-sided tape on and around the spot. ❧Sticky Paws XL® (PioneerPet.com) comes in 9-by-12-inch sheets and is safe for most carpets. Do not leave a single sheet on carpet or furniture for more than 30 days at a time.

• **Carpet protector.** Place a vinyl carpet runner, spiky side up, over the site. Some plastic car mats also have unpleasant spikes on the underside.

• **Strong scents.** Place something with strong odor on or near his target spot. Scented solid air fresheners work best; sprays and plug-ins don't smell intense enough. Try citrus, eucalyptus, citrus carpet cleaners, heavily scented potpourri (make sure cats can't come into direct contact with it), overpowering perfume or cologne. Don't use essential oils or liquid potpourri, as these are toxic to kitties and could burn Fluffy's mouth or skin.

• **Repellent sprays.** They have a strong repellent smell only while they're wet. You must refresh (or re-stink) the area daily. Repellents aren't impenetrable force fields; some cats may not be bothered by them. Don't use repellents near your kitty's food or litter box. Wait until it's dry before allowing your cat or other pets to go near the area. ⚠You may not like the smell either.

• **Rearrange the furniture so that the cat's favorite targets are inaccessible.**

• **Put his food and water dishes on the freshly cleaned soiled spot.** Cats don't want to eliminate near their food. But of course, some will. This won't work if he has too many spots in one room.

• **Plastic sheet.** After cleaning, covering a large area with a shower curtain may repel some cats. (Wait until the carpet and pad have completely dried to prevent mildew.) ⚠Some kitties actually prefer to pee on plastic.

• **Aluminum foil.** Lay foil over the place. Foil makes crackling noises when he steps on it. Besides, nobody likes splashback.

❧ **Comfort Zone with Feliway®.** (PetComfortZone.com) Dr. Buffington suggests this because cats seldom eliminate in areas where facial pheromones have been deposited. Don't spray Feliway in or next to the litter box.

• **Mothballs.** Put mothballs in an old pantyhose leg and place it (out of reach) above the formerly soiled area. [WARNING!] Make sure cats, dogs and kids can't get to it, because they are toxic.

• **Water.** If your cat pees or poops in the lavatory, leave a few inches of standing water in the bathtub or the basin.

Leave the deterrents in place in target areas until he's proven he's been rehabilitated.

Plant Problems

Fluffy enjoys watering your plants because soil is nature's cat litter. When I have to bring my plants inside for the winter, inevitably the cats think I have provided them with a lot of really neat new litter boxes. To keep your inside plants safe:
• Cover the planter with chicken wire or hardware cloth.
• Place stones, gravel, pine cones or orange peels on top of the dirt.
• Use cat deterrent sprays.

Making Corrections While He's in Lockup

While Fluffy is in detention, you'll have time to make adjustments around your home. We'll try the quick fixes first before we move on to more complicated options.
• Make sure everyone has been spayed/neutered.
• Remove the litter box hood.
• Switch to unscented, sandy clumping litter.
• Make different styles of litter available.
• Use a different style litter box than the one he's avoiding.

- Keep the litter about 2 inches deep.
- Scoop at least once or twice a day, and more often in multicat homes.
- One box per cat, plus one extra.
- Place a box on every floor of the house in easily accessible but low-traffic locations.
- Remove plastic carpet protectors and uncomfortable litter mats from the entrance of the box.
- If you've changed something about his box (litter brand, box style, location), change it back. (If you must move the box, once he's using it consistently, move it gradually or add a new one to the new spot.)
- Move food and water bowls and his bed away from the box.
- Stop using litter box liners.

Beyond commercial litter

It may take more than desirable litter to lure Fluffy back to his official toilet. Sometimes, when Fluffy avoids the litter box because of pain, bullying or disgust, he learns his alternative bathroom actually feels better against his paws than cat litter.

Consider your own flooring preferences when you go to the bathroom late at night. If you live in a cold climate, you likely prefer walking barefooted on carpet rather than tile because ceramic feels so cold against your skin. Think about how coarse, rocky gravel bruises your bare feet and how soothing wet sand feels between your toes.

Although cats usually head for softer textures like underwear and carpet, some prefer cool surfaces such as porcelain or linoleum. By peeing on soft textures, Fluffy may be telling you he'd favor soft litter in his box. Some cats pick a soft texture for pee and hard for poop. These kitties would probably appreciate a side-by-side soft/hard choice.

If you've had to replace carpet, hang on to some of those soiled remnants. A piece of stinky carpet in a different style litter box may be just the thing to help lure Fluffy back to the box.

When he begins to use the carpet inside the box, start adding ❀Cat Attract Cat Litter or ❀Senior Attract Cat Litter (PreciousCat.com) to the corners. As long as he continues to use the box, add a little more litter every day. Eventually the carpet or other texture will be covered by litter. When he's going on the litter, you can pull out the saturated, ugh, carpet, leaving behind only used cat litter.

Does he like to pee on the newspaper? Fill his box with shredded newspaper or ❀Carefresh Natural Pet Bedding (Healthy Pet®; Healthy-Pet.com; 800-242-2287), which is soft, fluffy critter bedding. Is the kitchen tile getting a workout? Try an empty litter box. Put whatever texture he's attracted to in his box, at least for a while.

Textures your kitty may prefer in the box may include:
- Carpet (soiled carpet, carpet squares)
- Freshly folded towels
- Dirty/clean clothes (T-shirt, underwear)
- Puppy pads
- Printer paper
- Old towels
- Cloth diapers
- Newspaper or cardboard
- Bed sheets
- Plastic trash/grocery bags
- Wood floor tile
- Sand or potting soil
- Bath mats
- An empty litter box

Turn the Soiled Spot into the Party Place

As I described in Chapter 13, hold catnip parties, play sessions, dining and spa experiences to change the context of rooms he's been marking or using as a toilet.

Cats in Counseling

If none of your efforts can persuade your cat to return to the litter box or stop him from spray painting with yellow pigment, you may need to call in a kitty shrink. A cat behaviorist can come to your home and objectively observe your cat's behavior, the layout of the house and family dynamics, and devise a strategy. Make sure to talk to someone with extensive experience in feline behavior. Behaviorists are not created equal. Only four organizations certify cat behavior specialists. Although self-taught behavior consultants can be knowledgeable, there's no guarantee that they have been trained in effective behavior techniques. Many old-school methods touted on the Internet can do more harm than good. If you're lucky enough to have a vet school nearby, ask if they have a behavior clinic.

American College of Veterinary Behaviorists (DACVB.org): A veterinary behaviorist is a licensed veterinarian who can prescribe medication.

American Veterinary Society of Animal Behavior (AVMA.org/avsab/default.htm)

Certified Applied Animal Behaviorist (CAAB or ACAAB): A certified applied animal behaviorist (CAAB or ACAAB) generally has a PhD in animal behavior. (AnimalBehaviorSociety.org)

International Association of Animal Behavior Consultants (IAABC): Members of IAABC must display a minimum knowledge of science-based behavior and participate in continuing education. (IAABC.org)

When all else fails... what to do next?

16   WHEN ALL ELSE FAILS

Patience and perseverance have a magical effect before which difficulties disappear and obstacles vanish. ~ John Quincy Adams

Sometimes, no matter how hard you work or what you try, you, your vet and your cat behaviorist just can't solve Fluffy's (or multiple Fluffies') marking or peeing problem. So now what? Do you accept his shortcomings and make adjustments in the house to minimize the smell and mess, find him a new home, surrender him to a shelter, or put him to sleep? Here are some options to consider before you resort to euthanasia.

Coping Options

If, in your mind, Fluffy is forever and rehoming, relinquishment or euthanasia are not options, good for you. You can try some tricks to reduce or eliminate odor and control the mess. The cost of options runs the gambit from free to very expensive. I think it goes without saying that expensive will probably be more effective than free.

• **Cardboard sheet:** Big box stores such as Sam's and Costco present stock on wooden pallets, with stock layers separated by 4-by-4-foot cardboard dividers. For kitties who go in predictable locations, free and thoroughly unattractive cardboard makes an effective pee shield. Place a plastic sheet (trash bag or shower curtain) beneath it to prevent pee from reaching the carpet. On garbage day, fold it and throw it away.

❀ **Drymate® Potty Training Mate**; (DryMate.com) is designed for potty training puppies with much higher bladder capacity. It contains mess. It's machine washable.

❀ **Drymate® Cat Litter Mat** has a non-woven fabric facing with a bonded waterproof backing. The fabric is highly absorptive, so there is no pee runoff, and the backing prevents leak-through. It is washable in cool water and dryer safe at low heat. It works on either carpeting or hard flooring.

• **Waterproof and washable furniture protection:** Washable ❀Surefit furniture slipcovers (Sure Fit; SureFit.net; 888-796-0500) prevent pee from saturating cushions. Fabulous. Take them off when company arrives.

• **Puppy pads**

• **Washable and reusable fabric nursing home pee pads**

• **Put your cat in cat diapers.** Diapers may keep the pee off your walls, but like a baby wearing a diaper, you must constantly monitor the diaper for new contents. When worn around the clock, most of them force the cat to poop inside the diaper. (Not cool. You'll have to bathe him every time he goes to the bathroom.) Best practice is to take it off every couple of hours to let the kitty potty in a confined area. If you leave it on when wet or dirty, your cat will suffer ammonia burns. (You can buy specially designed cat diapers at HandicappedPets.com.)

Feline Friendly Flooring

If your cat has been anointing the carpet for a long time, you may have to throw in the towel and replace your current flooring. If you have to replace the carpet, consider flooring that will make kitty crimes an easy clean-up, something impervious to pee and odor such as stone, ceramic tile or vinyl.

Before installing new flooring, treat the subfloor with hydrogen peroxide as I also described in Chapter 7 Crime Scene Cleanup. When it's completely dry, seal it. The experts I spoke with recommended sealing the floor with ❀Kilz® Max Stain and Odor Blocker (Masterchem Industries; Kilz.com; 866-977-3711). Treat the walls and baseboards, too.

Consider replacing your current floor with fire-glazed ceramic tile. Add ❀Grout Boost® (H.B. Fuller Construction Products Inc.; GroutBoost.com; 800-832-9002) additive to cement-based grout in place of water when grout is installed to provide resistance to water and oil-based grout stains.

Avoid:

• **Wood:** Odors can accumulate because you just can't get up every trace of pee. However, you can seal wood floors with two coats of ❀ Fabulon (Essex Silver-Line Corp; Essex-Silver-Line.com; 978-957-6989), a polyurethane coating similar to bowling alley floors. If the finish can stand up to spilled beer and dropped bowling balls, it can stand up to cat pee. Marion Lane, who was the special projects editor for the national office of the ASPCA, said Fabulon worked fabulously. Cat pee beads up and wipes away clean.

• **Laminate:** Even laminate flooring is less than ideal because it can't be sealed. If pee isn't cleaned up right away, it will seep between the planks causing them to swell. The planks are then ruined.

• **Self-sticking linoleum or vinyl tile squares:** These may work better than carpet and wood, but if not placed correctly, they can work loose when pee collects beneath tiles.

• **Carpet:** Cats and carpets don't mix. When it comes time to replace the carpet—don't. Carpeting is difficult to care for under the best of circumstances. Add the three Ps (pee, poop and puke) and it becomes an olfactory nightmare.

• **Natural stone:** It is porous and absorbs pee odors.

• **Unhoned marble:** It is also very porous.

Give Him a Room of His Own

Dr. Buffington suggested giving cats their own room or large freestanding (bird) cage.

"We have done both of these before with some success," he said.

If you have a spare room, consider converting it into the kitty's own personal sanctuary. A private room of his own would provide Fluffy with protection from other pets, as well as safeguard your floor throughout the house.

Your kitty's private quarters can be a safe and interesting place to eat, sleep and play. Cat proof the floor as I suggested early in this chapter. Install a screen door so you can keep him separate without him feeling he's been shipped off to Siberia.

Set up opportunities for Fluffy to hide, perch, observe, and play. Dressers and bookcases can double as elevated perches and cardboard boxes will give him a place to hide. Outfit the room with food, water, a scratcher and multiple litter boxes because you want to encourage proper litter box habits. [WARNING!] Keep Fluffy's bathrooms well away from his food and water bowls.

Provide food-puzzles to stimulate his hunting instincts and make his life more interesting. Also lay out treasure hunts to help him pass the time when you aren't around. Motion-activated toys or trackballs also give solo cats something to do. If he's not agitated by outside animals, set up a chair next to a window or place a towel on the window sill. Make sure you have a love seat or chair so you can keep your cat company while you read, watch TV or do crosswords.

Make Him an Indoor/Outdoor Cat

Instead of thinking inside the box, it may be time to think outside the house. In some police and military dramas they offer the criminals the chance to go on a dangerous mission, and if they survive, they stay free. In a sense, if you simply open your door, that's what you're offering Fluffy.

This option certainly has its downsides. There's no question, outdoor cats do face hazards (cars, predators, cruel people, disease and other aggressive cats). The average lifespan for an inside-only cat is 14 to 18 years, whereas for an inside/outside cat it is only 4 to 8.

On the upside, many cats who are stressed by 24/7 inside life respond well once when they're given more freedom. In some cats, feline interstitial cystitis (FIC) and elimination problems completely resolve by letting him become an indoor/outdoor cat.

Going outside doesn't have to mean releasing him to the elements. Enclose your yard with a cat fence. Personally, I've used other brands but I've have the best luck with ❧Affordable Cat Fence (catfence.com), which attaches to an existing wood or chain link fence. ❧Purr...fect® Fence (PurrfectFence.com) offers a freestanding cat fence for unfenced yards. ❧ C & D Pet Products sells pre-built cat enclosure kits that only need to be bolted together. You could also try enclosing a porch. Don't forget to update his rabies and feline leukemia vaccinations.

Rehome Your Cat

Some problems can't be resolved if circumstances within the home don't change. You may not be able to stop your kid from antagonizing the cat. Your timid cat may not be able to function in a large multicat home. In these situations, rehoming the cat may be your best option. It's not unusual for a kitty who has been stressed in one environment to thrive in another, calmer setting or in a home with fewer felines.

Once the trouble maker is gone you can get a new, better cat. Right? Maybe. But a new cat is going to enter the same home with the same dynamics, as well as the same soiled carpets and walls. Don't be surprised if the new cat becomes "broken" as well. If you have to rehome a cat, leave it at that. Don't push your luck by expanding your feline population.

Rehoming options include:

• **Return him to where you got him.** If you got your kitty from a breeder, an animal shelter or a rescue organization, check your paperwork. Hopefully, there will be a provision reading something like, "If you can no longer keep him, you are required to return the cat to our organization." Let the breeder and shelter know that you may need to return the cat. Don't call them today and expect to be free of him tomorrow. They will need time to arrange a place for your cat.

• **Ask a friend.** If you don't have a return option, do you have a friend who might be willing to help? If Fluffy is introduced slowly to the new home with good litter box care, it may be a happy union.

• **Ask a rescue group to help you find a home.** Go to your nearby pet supply stores on the weekend to meet the humane organizations holding adoption events to see if they can take your kitty. Meet with the cat rescue coordinator. Explain your situation and ask if you can place the cat in the organization's program. Offer to foster the cat until he is adopted. The coordinator will probably require that the cat be neutered, be current on his shots, wormed, and tested for feline leukemia and feline immunodeficiency virus. You'll most likely be expected to bring him to adoption events and pick him up when the event is over if he hasn't found a home.

[WARNING!] Do not put him on Craig's List or give him away free unless you personally know the family. While not everyone who gets an animal from Craig's List is a perv, many use the website to acquire live bait to train fighting dogs or to feed large snakes or simply to abuse animals in unspeakable ways. Better to euthanize him than to subject him to a short life of torture.

Casually ask potential adopters lots of questions. Don't interrogate them. You'll get more information if you're friendly and conversational. Evasive or vague answers about where they live, other pets, what happened to past pets or a vet's contact information raise red flags. Questions include:

• Do you have pets? Sympathetically ask what happened to past pets.

- Does your dog get along with cats?
- Are they inside or outside pets?
- Who's your vet? Take time to contact the clinic. The vet may not release information, but you might be able to glean something by the person's tone or hesitation. If the potential adopter was a responsible cat owner, the office staff would probably be glad to tell you. Ask the person if she'd allow the client to adopt one of her personal pets.

You can even do a cheap background check online.

Follow your gut. If you feel uncomfortable at any point, stop the process. Stay safe and only let responsible, kind people take your cat. Believe me, there are wackos out there. You aren't obligated to hand over your cat just because someone shows interest. You can even charge an adoption fee.

Surrender him to a shelter

If you surrender him to a shelter, be honest with the staff about Fluffy's shortcomings. You don't want him to bounce from home to home or suffer future abuse because of his problem.

Barn cat

If you've been unsuccessful in your quest to find Fluffy an inside home, contact shelters and rescue groups in your area about feral cat or barn cat relocation organizations. You can get more information about this at Barn Cats Inc. (BarnCats.org), Alley Cat Allies (AlleyCatAllies.org) or Alley Cat Rescue (SaveACat.org). Understand that even under the best circumstances, barn cats can fall victim to predators. This isn't a good option for declawed, elderly or sick cats.

Drug therapy

I consider this to be a last resort alternative to euthanasia, especially for clients who only want to change the cat, not the context.

In her presentation "Feline Inappropriate Elimination" at the Latin American Veterinary Conference in 2008, Terry M. Curtis said, "Most cases of inappropriate elimination are treated and resolved with environmental modification alone and medication is not needed." However, in some stress-related cases your behaviorist or vet may conclude your kitty might benefit from short-term antianxiety meds.

Drug therapy isn't usually prescribed for kitties who pee outside the litter box unless the cat is too frightened or anxious to approach his bathroom—for example, if the bookshelf fell off the wall while Fluffy was taking a pee or another cat terrorizes him. Because all medications have potential side effects, and cats usually respond without meds, try the other methods in the book before doping him.

Unless your behaviorist is also a vet, she'll have to work with your own vet to come up with the drug treatment that's the safest and most effective for your particular case. In most cases, drug therapy is recommended to assist in behavioral modification and training, but doesn't replace them. In other words, the drugs never work alone. The purpose behind giving any or all of these medications is to stabilize the cat's mood and reduce anxiety, so that the other changes you are making will be more effective.

Euthanasia

If you've done everything possible, and your home is unhealthy, you're not happy and the cat's not happy, it may be time to consider humane euthanasia. For your own peace of mind, exhaust all other strategies before you resort to this option. Ultimately, you want to have no regrets. Speak with your vet. If Fluffy is constantly in pain due to FIC or another health issue, euthanasia may be a kind option.

If you decide on euthanasia, don't rush to action. Speak with your vet and then take a few days to think it over. You may change your mind.

You Can Do It!

I've covered a lot of ideas and options in this book. Your to-do list may seem impossibly long. Everything feels overwhelming. How can you accomplish so many things to do all at the same time?

As I've said throughout the book, start with a deep breath, then take your cat to the vet. Bring him home and isolate him. Give him an attractive box, or multiple boxes in safe, easy-to-access locations. Fill it with comfortable litter and clean it every day. Make his target locations unattractive.

As a new morning routine, get up, go to the bathroom, flush your own toilet (think how disgusting your toilet would be if you only flushed it once a day— worse still—every couple of days). While your coffee is brewing, scoop the box. It only takes 15 seconds. Afterward, neither you nor Fluffy will have to smell cat pee or poop. Scoop once more when you get home from work, and maybe before you go to bed. You're happier because you don't have to smell a dirty litter box. Fluffy is happier because he has a freshly flushed toilet. There are no excuses for not doing it.

You can turn this around, but it takes patience and persistence. Simply keep moving forward, even when it feels like it would be easier to give up. Just take everything one step at a time. This is doable.

READER RESOURCES

Environmental Enrichment
The Indoor Cat Initiative. Ohio State University. Dr. Tony Buffington.
http://indoorpet.osu.edu/cats

How to Clean a Litter Box
Lisa A. Pierson, DVM.
https://www.youtube.com/watch?v=SeFDKUga5Bc

Multicat Homes
Cat Wrangling Made Easy: Maintaining Peace and Sanity in Your Multicat Home. The Lyons Press. 2007. Dusty Rainbolt. Second edition published by Stupid Gravity Press, LLC in Feb 2017.

Cat/Dog Relationships
Fit Dog: Tips and Tricks to Give Your Pet a Longer, Healthier, Happier Life, especially chapter 9. Arden Moore. Firefly Books. 2015

ComPETability: Solving Behavior Problems in Your CAT-DOG Household. Amy D. Shojai. FurryMuse Publications. 2012.

Handicapped and incontinent pets
HandicappedPets.com

Toxoplasmosis
http://www.cdc.gov/parasites/toxoplasmosis/gen_info/faqs.html

General Cat Information
Outsmarting Cats: How To Persuade The Felines In Your Life To Do What You Want. Wendy Christensen. Lyons Press. 2013

SELECTED WORKS CITED

American Association of Feline Practitioners/Academy of Feline Medicine Panel Report on Feline Senior Care". Journal of Feline Medicine and Surgery. Nov. 23, 2004. (20050 7, 3-32. doic 10.1016/j.fms.2004.04.004. http://jfm.sagepub.com/content/7/1/3.extract. http://www.vin.com/Members/SearchDB/misc/m05000/m04855.htm

American Association of Feline Practitioners. "Feline Diabetes." http://www.catvets.com/cat-owners/disease-and-conditions/flutd

Adelman, Beth, CCBC. Phone and email interviews. Reach her at Facebook.com/beth.heidi?fref=ts

Alanbrooke and Danchev, Alex. War Diaries, 1939-1945: Field Marshall Lord Alanbrooke. University of California Press. May 5, 2003.

Bamberger, Michelle, MS, DVM; Houpt, Katherine A, VMD, PhD, DACVB. "Signalment factors, comorbidity, and trends in behavior diagnoses in cats: 736 cases (1991–2001)". JAVMA, Vol 229, No. 10, Nov. 15, 2006. Pg 1606.

Becker, Marty, DVM. "The tragedy of post-declaw pain syndrome, and how to help cats who suffer from it." http://www.drmartybecker.com/veterinary-medicine/the-tragedy-of-post-declaw-pain-syndrome-and-how-to-help-cats-who-suffer-from-it/ Dec. 11, 2015.

Blagburn, Byron L, MS, PhD. "Problems associated with intestinal parasites in cats". DVM360.com. May 1, 2002. http://veterinarynews.dvm360.com/dvm/article/articleDetail.jsp?id=173 45&sk=&date=&pageID=2

Blagburn, Byron, MS, PhD. "Zoonotic diseases." CVC in San Diego Proceedings. Oct. 1, 2008. http://veterinarycalendar.dvm360.com/avhc/article/articleDetail.jsp?id= 581746&pageID=1&sk=&date=

Brooks, Wendy C, DVM, DipABVP. "Giardia". The Pet Health Library. Educational Director, VeterinaryPartner.com http://www.veterinarypartner.com/Content.plx?P=A&S=0&C=0&A=2386

Brutlag, Ahna, DVM, MS, DABT, DABVT. Associate director of veterinary services, director of consulting services & adjunct assistant professor at the Department of Veterinary and Biomedical Sciences at the College of Veterinary Medicine, University of Minnesota St. Paul, MN. Pet Poison Helpline & SafetyCall International, PLLC. Email interview.

Buffington, Tony.
http://indoorpet.osu.edu/cats/basicneeds/litterboxes/index.cfm

Buffington. C.A. Tony, DVM, PhD, DACVN. "Pandora syndrome: Rethinking our approach to idiopathic cystitis in cats."
http://veterinarymedicine.dvm360.com/pandora-syndrome-rethinking-our-approach-idiopathic-cystitis-cats

Buffington, C. A. Tony, DVM, PhD, DACVN email interview Aug. 25, 2014 and phone interviews

Buffington, C. A. Tony, DVM, PhD, DACVN. "External and internal influences on disease risk in cats." JAVMA, Vol 220, No. 7, April 1, 2002. P 994-1002. http://www.vet.ohio-state.edu/assets/pdf/education/courses/vcs724/lectures/buffington/reference.pdf

Center for Disease Control and Prevention. "Toxoplasmosis: An Important Message for Cat Owners".
www.cdc.gov/ncidod/dpd/parasites/toxoplasmosis/factsht_toxoplasmosis.htm

Centers for Disease Control and Prevention. "Toxoplasmosis: An Important Message for Cat Owners".
http://www.cdc.gov/parasites/toxoplasmosis/resources/printresources/catowners.pdf

Chew, Dennis, DVM, DACVIM; Buffington, C.A. Tony, DVM, PhD, DACVN "CVC Highlight: How to think outside the litter box: Managing cats with nonobstructive idiopathic interstitial cystitis". Dec 1, 2009.
http://veterinarymedicine.dvm360.com/cvc-highlight-how-think-outside-litter-box-managing-cats-with-nonobstructive-idiopathic-interstitial?rel=canonical

Cohen, Elizabette, DVM. Phone interview.
Cornell Feline Health Center. "Toxoplasmosis in Cats."
http://www.vet.cornell.edu/fhc/Health_Information/brochure_toxo.cfm .

Cornell Feline Health Center. "Hyperthyroidism in Cats.
http://www.vet.cornell.edu/fhc/Health_Information/brochure_hyperthyr
oid.cfm

Cornell Feline Health Center. "Inflammatory Bowel Disease."
http://www.vet.cornell.edu/fhc/health_information/brochure_ibd.cfm

Cornell Feline Health Center. "Feline Lower Urinary Tract Disease."
http://www.vet.cornell.edu/FHC/health_information/UrinaryConcerns.cf
m

Cornell Feline Health Center. "The Special Needs of the Senior Cat."
http://www.vet.cornell.edu/FHC/health_information/brochure_seniorcat.
cfm

Cornell Feline Health Center. "Feline Diabetes."
http://www.vet.cornell.edu/FHC/health_resources/diabetes.cfm

Crowell-Davis, Sharon, DVM, PhD, DACVB. "Educating Clients To Prevent
Feline Behavioral Problems." The North American Veterinary Conference.
Proceeding of the NAVC North American Veterinary Conference. Jan. 8-12,
2005. Orlando, FL.
http://www.ivis.org/proceedings/navc/2005/SAE/032.pdf?LA=1

Curtis, Terry Marie, DVM, MS, DACVB. "Feline Housesoiling." NAVC
Clinician's Brief. Applied Behavior. May2012. Pgs 19-22.

Curtis, Terry Marie, DVM, MS, Diplomate ACVB. "Feline Inappropriate
Urination". Today's Veterinary Practice. Sept./Oct. 2015.
http://216.119.71.215/mags/1509/T1509C05.pdf

Curtis, Terry. "Feline Inappropriate Elimination." Proceeding of the Latin
American Veterinary Conference Oct. 3-6, 2008 – Lima, Peru

DeLeon, Fernando. "Dealing with Litter Box Problems".
http://www.docstoc.com/docs/13287600/Litterbox-Problems---Animal-

Trustees-of-Austin

Dodman, Nicholas H., BVMS, MRCVS. Phone and email interviews.

Dodman, Nicholas H. "Feline Urine Marking".

Dodman, Nicholas H. "Feline Inappropriate Elimination". Owner info sheet.

Dodman, Nicholas H. "Inter-Cat Territorial Aggression". July 27, 2015. http://blog.halopets.com/2015/07/27/inter-cat-territorial-aggression

V. Dramard; L. Kern, J. Hofmans; C. Halsberghe; C.A. Rème. "Clinical efficacy of L-theanine tablets to reduce anxiety-related emotional disorders in cats: A pilot open-label clinical trial." Journal of Veterinary Behavior. http://www.journalvetbehavior.com/article/S1558-7878%2807%2900091-3/abstract http://www.virbacvet.com/pdf/product_pdfs/ANXITANE_L_theanine_Che wable_Tablets_Label_Clinical_Trial.pdf>>>>

Dijkstra, Pieter U, PhD; Geertzen, Jan H.B , PhD; Stewart, Roy, MSc; Van der Schans, Cees P, PhD. "Phantom Pain and Risk Factors." Journal of Pain and Symptom Management. Dec. 2002. Volume 24, Issue 6, Pgs 578–585

Easterly, Susan. "Cats that Lick Too Much". http://www.vet.cornell.edu/fhc/health_resources/CW_lick.cfm

Eckstein, Sandy. "Feline Diabetes: Symptoms, Treatments, Prevention, and Diet Tips." http://pets.webmd.com/cats/guide/feline-diabetes-symptoms-treatments-prevention-diet

Everson, Kim, DVM. "The ABC's of Anal Glands." Oct. 9, 2011. http://petvet1.blogspot.com/2011/10/abcs-of-anal-glands.html

Ewing, Tom. Dec. 20, 2010. "Diagnosis: Kidney Disease" . http://www.vet.cornell.edu/FHC/health_ resources/kidneydisease.cfm
Ewing, Tom. "Constipation". http://www.vet.cornell.edu/fhc/health_resources/constipation.cfm

Forrester, S. Dru, DVM, MS, DACVIM. "How Important is It?" Proceedings 2007 Hill's FLUTD Symposium, Feline Lower Urinary Tract Disease: Thinking Outside (and Inside) the Litter Box.

Forrester, S. Dru, DVM, MS, DACVIM. "FLUTD: Are You Choosing the Right Therapy? Part 2." Feline Idiopathic Cystitis, Proceedings of the 2007 Hill's FLUTD Symposium, Feline Lower Urinary Tract Disease: Thinking Outside (and Inside) the Litter Box.

Fry, Jennifer L. VMD. "Anal Glands—Why is My Pet Scooting?" http://www.drfry.biz/rich_text_1.html

Golon, Caroline. TheHappyLitterBox.com. "Your Senior Cat and the Litter Box." www.thehappylitterbox.com/2011/03/your-senior-cat-and-the-litter-box

Grauer, Gregory F, DVM, MS, DACVIM. "New thoughts about chronic kidney disease". CVC In Kansas City proceedings. Aug. 1, 2010. http://veterinarycalendar.dvm360.com/new-thoughts-about-chronic-kidney-disease-part-1-proceedings

Guinness World Records. "Oldest Living Cat." http://www.guinnessworldrecords.com/world-records/oldest-cat-living

Gunn-Moore, Danièlle A, PhD. "Cognitive Dysfunction in Cats: Clinical Assessment and Management." http://www.companimalmed.com/article/S1938-9736%2811%2900007-9/abstract?cc=y

Gunn-Moore, DA; Cameron, ME. "A pilot study using synthetic feline facial pheromone for the management of feline idiopathic cystitis." Journal of Feline Medicine and Surgery. (2004) 6, 133–138

Hardie EM; Roe SC; Martin FR. "Radiographic evidence of degenerative joint disease in geriatric cats:100 cases (1994-1997)". JAVMA 220:628-632, 200211. http://www.tibma.net/pubs/Inappropriate_elimination.pdf
Hardie, Elizabeth M, DVM, PhD. "Management of Osteoarthritis in Cats". Veterinary Clinics: Small Animal Practice. July 1997 Volume 27, Issue 4, PagesPgs 945–953.

Hart BL; Barrett RE. "Effects of castration on fighting, roaming and urine spraying in adult male cats." JAVMA 163:290-292, 1973. http://www.tibma.net/pubs/Inappropriate_elimination.pdf

Hess-Fischl, Amy MS, RD, LDN, BC-ADM, CDE. "What is Insulin?" Indocrineweb.com. http://www.endocrineweb.com/conditions/type-1-diabetes/what-insulin

Horwitz, Debra F, DVM, DACVB. "The Link Between House Soiling and Feline Intercat Aggression." Proceedings of the Australian Veterinary Association (AVA) Annual Conferences, 2012 AVA Annual Conference, Canberra, Behaviour, May 2012

Hovda, Lynn Rolland RPh, DVM, MS, DACVIM. Email interview via Katie Michels info@petpoisonhelpline.com

Huston, Lorie, DVM. Phone and email interviews.

Johnson, Karen DVM interview.

Johnson-Bennet. Pam. "Turn an Outdoor Cat into an Indoor Cat." http://www.catbehaviorassociates.com/making-an-outdoor-cat-into-an-indoor-cat/

Johnson-Bennet. Pam. "Cat Has Loose Stool (Feline Diarrhea)." http://www.catbehaviorassociates.com/litter-box-aversion-is-it-medical-or-behavioral/

Jones. Cynthia. "Diagnosing Cat Litter Box Issues: A Focus on Disease and the Aging Feline". Fall 2004. http://zimmer-foundation.org/sch/cjb.html

Koski, Marci, PhD. Feline Behavior Solutions. Phone interviews.
William Kristol. "Men at War." The Weekly Standard. Jan. 23, 2012, Vol. 17, No. 18. http://www.weeklystandard.com/articles/men-war_616727.html

Kruger, JM; Osborne, CA; Goyal, SM, et al. "Clinical evaluation of cats with lower urinary tract disease." JAVMA 1991;199:211–216.

Landsberg, Gary M; Nichol, Jeff; Araujo, Joseph A. "Cognitive Dysfunction Syndrome. Vet Clinic Small Animals 42 (2012) 749 –768; http://dx.doi.org/10.1016/j.cvsm.2012.04.003; vetsmall.theclinics.com; 0195-5616/12 http://webinars.veteducation.com.au/wp-content/images/Cognitive-Dysfunction-Syndrome.pdf Pgs 749-768. gmlandvm@aol.com

Landsberg, Gary M, BSc DVM MRCVS DACVB DECVBM-CA; Denenberg, Sagi, DVM MACVSc; Araujo, Joseph A. "Cognitive Dysfunction in Cats: A Syndrome we Used to Dismiss as 'Old Age.'" http://jfm.sagepub.com/content/12/11/837.short .

Levitan, Diane, VMD, Dip ACVIM, owner of Mobile Veterinary Ultrasound & Endoscopy in Long Island. Interview.

Little, Susan, DVM, Diplomate ABVP (Feline Practice). "A Practical Approach to Feline Housesoiling".

Luescher, AU. "Compulsive Behavior in Companion Animals." http://www.2ndchance.info/acral-Luescher2000.pdf appearing in Recent Advances in Companion Animal Behavior Problems. Houpt K.A.; (Ed.). International Veterinary Information Service, Ithaca NY.

Mauger, Jennifer, CPDT-KSA. Certified professional dog trainer, and feline behavior consultant from Akron, OH. Owner of L'Chaim Feline www.lchaimfeline.com. Phone and email interviews.

Mayo Clinic. "Arthritis." http://www.mayoclinic.org/diseases-conditions/arthritis/basics/definition/con-20034095

Nagelschneider, Mieshelle. Cat behaviorist at the www.thecatBehavior clinic.com in Portland and author of The Cat Whisperer. Phone and email interviews.

Neilson, Jacqueline C., DVM, DACVB. "Thinking Outside The Box: Feline Elimination." J Feline Med Surg 6[1]:5-11 Feb 2004 Review Article 20 Refs; http://www.vin.com/Members/SearchDB/journals/scanned/ja022500/ja021298.htm

Neilson, Jacqueline C, DVM. "Feline House Soiling: Elimination and Marking Problems." Clinical Techniques in Small Animal Practice. Oct. 2004. Pgs. 216-224. http://www.tibma.net/pubs/Inappropriate_elimination.pdf

Neilson, Jacqueline C, DVM, DACVB; "The latest scoop on litter;" March 1, 2009; http://veterinarymedicine.dvm360.com/vetmed/Feline+Center/The-latest-scoop-on-litter/ArticleStandard/Article/detail/584615

Neilson, Jacqueline C, DVM, DACVB. "FLUTD: When Should You Call the Behaviorist?" Proceedings of the 2007 Hill's FLUTD Symposium, Feline Lower Urinary Tract Disease: Thinking Outside (and Inside) the Litter Box.

Neilson, Jacqueline C, DVM. "Feline House Soiling: Elimination and Marking Behaviors". Veterinary Clinics of North America: Small Animal Practice 33(2):287-301, 2003. 1096-2867/04/$-see http://www.tibma.net/pubs/Inappropriate_elimination.pdf

Nelson, Thomas, DVM. Phone and email interviews. http://www.knowheartworms.org/nelson.asp
Nestor, Kim. Cat behaviorist, Pasadena Humane Society & SPCA phone interview 2013

Ogata, Niwako. "Feline Urine Marking & Inter-cat Aggression". World Small Animal Vet Association World Congress Proceedings 2001;, Japan. http://www.vin.com/Members/Proceedings/Proceedings.plx?CID=wsava 2001&PID=pr00029&O=VIN

Ogata, Niwako. 9-16-2015 phone interview, BVSc, PhD, DACVB. Asst Professor, Companion Animal Behavior. Dept. Veterinary Clinical Sciences. College of Veterinary Medicine, Purdue University, 625 Harrison St., West Lafayette, IN.

Olah, Glenn Allen, DVM, DABVP (Feline), PhD. "Top 5 Ways to Enrich Feline Environmental Needs," Sept. 2014 Issue Veterinary Team Brief. http://www.veterinaryteambrief.com/article/top-5-ways-enrich-feline-environmental-needs?utm_medium=email&utm_source=Veterinary+Team+Brief+eNewsl etter&utm_campaign=VTB+ENL+SEPT+30+2014

Ortiz-Catalan, Max; Sander, Nichlas; Kristoffersen, Morten B; Håkansson, Bo; Brånemark, Rickard. "Treatment of phantom limb pain (PLP) based on augmented reality and gaming controlled by myoelectric pattern recognition: a case study of a chronic PLP patient." Front. Neurosci., (25) Feb. 25, 2014 | http://dx.doi.org/10.3389/fnins.2014.00024. http://journal.frontiersin.org/article/10.3389/fnins.2014.00024/full

Overall KL. "Feline elimination disorders." Clinical Behavioral Medicine for Small Animals. St. Louis, Mosby, 1997, Pgs 160-194.

Overall, Karen L, MA, VMD, PhD, DACVB, ABS Certified Applied Animal Behaviorist. "Associations Between Feline Elimination and Aggression Disorders."

Patronek GJ. "Assessment of Claims of Short and Long Term Complications Associated with Onychectomy in Cats." JAVMA 219(7):932-937, 2001. PetMD.com. Anal Sac Problems in Cats http://pets.webmd.com/cats/anal-sac-problems-cats

PetMD.com. Constipation in Cats. http://www.petmd.com/cat/conditions/digestive/c_ct_constipation_obsti pation

PetMD.com. "Constipation (Severe) in Cats." htp://www.petmd.com/cat/conditions/digestive/c_ct_megacolon

PetMD.com. "Constipation in Cats." http://www.petmd.com/cat/emergency/common-emergencies/e_ct_constipation

PetPlace.com. "Selegiline HCl (Anipryl®, Eldepryl®) for Dogs and Cats." http://www.petplace.com/article/drug-library/library/prescription/selegiline-hcl-anipryl

Pierson, Lisa A, DVM. "The Litter Box From Your Cat's Point of View." www.catinfo.org/litterbox.htm#Top_reasons_for_a_cat_to_stop_using_his_l itter_box

Pierson, Lisa A, DVM. "Feline Hyperthyroidism." http://www.catinfo.org/?link=felinehyperthyroidism

Pierson, Lisa A, DVM. http://www.catinfo.org/?link=litterbox#Cleaning_the_Litter_Box:

Plotnick, Arnold, MS, DVM, ACVIM, ABVP. "Cognitive Dysfunction Syndrome in Cats." http://www.manhattancats.com/Articles/CDS.html

Plotnick, Arnold, MS, DVM, ACVIM, ABVP. Feline Lifestages Chart. http://www.manhattancats.com/Articles/CDS.html

Pryor PA; Hart BL; Bain MJ; Cliff KD. "Causes of urine marking in cats and

effects of environmental management on frequency of marking." JAVMA 219:1709-1713, 2001 (http://www.ncbi.nlm.nih.gov/pubmed/11767919)
Rainbolt, Dusty, ACCBC. "Stress in Cats".
http://dustycatwriter.com/nv_dusty/2015/02/22/stress-cats

Rajewski, Genevieve. "The Hurt Unlocker."
http://now.tufts.edu/articles/pets-in-pain

Robins, Sandy. "Body and Mind." http://www.petage.com/body-and-mind/

M. Salman, J.Hutchison, R. Ruch-Gallie, L. Kogan, J. New, P. Kass, J Scarlett. "Behavioral Reasons for Relinquishment of Dogs and Cats to 12 Shelters." Journal of Applied Animal Welfare Science, 3(2), 93–106. 2000.

Email interview with Margie Scherk, DVM, DABVP (feline practice) March 18, 2016

Schultz, Jacque Lynn CPDT. Transitioning an Outdoor Cat to Indoors.
https://www.petfinder.com/cats/cat-care/transitioning-outdoor-cat/

Shojai, Amy, CABC. http://cats.about.com/od/amyshojai/a/7-Tips-for-Solving-Old-Cat-Litter-Box-Problems.htm

Siracusa, Carlo, DVM, MS, PhD. Director of Penn Vet's Animal Behavior Service. Phone interview.

Sparkes, Andy, BVetMedPhD DipECVIMMRCVS. "Feline idiopathic cystitis: Epidemiology, risk factors and pathogenesis."
http://www.hillsvet.com/HillsVetUS/v1/portal/en/us/content/research/FLUTH_Urolithisasis/Feline_idiopathic-cystitis_Epidemiology_FLUTH-Symposium_2014.pdf
Crosby, Janet Tobiassen, DVM. "Anipryl® - Help for Senior Dogs?"
http://vetmedicine.about.com/cs/diseasesall/a/aniprylseniors.htm Dec. 18, 2014.

Vance, Kristen, DVM Homeward Bound Mobile Vet. Bel Air, MD. Email interview.

Vetinfo.com. "Cholodin Feline Side Effects."
http://www.vetinfo.com/cholodin-feline-side-effects.html

Virga, Vint, DVM, Dipl ACVB. "Thinking Inside the Box: A Practical Approach to House Soiling Cats." Atlantic Coast Veterinary Conference 2002. Behavioral Medicine for Animals / Veterinary Healing Arts, Inc. New York, NY, USA / Newport, RI. http://www.vin.com/Members/Proceedings/Proceedings.plx?CID=acvc2 002&PID=pr02467&O=VIN. Feb 6, 2007.

Multiple interviews with Drew Weigner, DVM, ABVP at The Cat Doctor clinic in greater Atlanta area.

Westropp, Jodi L , DVM; Buffington, C.A. Tony, DVM, PhD. "Feline idiopathic cystitis: current understanding of pathophysiology and management." http://vet.osu.edu/assets/pdf/hospital/indoorcat/vcna041.pdf

Wright, John C, Ph.D. "How to Introduce an Adopted Cat to a New Household." Certified Applied Animal Behaviorist, Professor of Psychology. Mercer University, Macon, GA 31207

Yeon SC, Flanders JA, Scarlett JM, et al. "Attitudes of owners regarding tendonectomy and onychectomy in cats." JAVMA 218(1):43-47, 2001.

Silene Young, DVM. "Challenges in parasite management." DVM360.com. May 1, 2010. http://veterinarynews.dvm360.com/dvm/Parasitology+Center/Challenge s-in-parasite-management/ArticleStandard/Article/detail/ 666580?ref=25

Index

3-D environment, 60, 77, 145

A Box with a View, 75

Ace Hardware Super Tub, 29

active play, 66, 124, 145

acute renal failure, 136

affordable cat fence, 60, 157, 176

aggression, 105, 138

aggression, cause, 62, 73, 73, 87

aggression, intercat, 59, 73

aggression, redirected, 73, 87

aging cats, 99, 119, 121, 123, 126, 130

air freshener, 24, 27, 34, 39, 51, 62, 65, 168

Alley Cat Allies, 178

Alley Cat Rescue, 178

altering your cat, 57

ambush, 76, 79, 147

anal sac disease, 100, 101, 103

another pet, 9, 21, 87

antianxiety drugs, 62

arthritis, 33, 36, 101, 102, 123, 126, 127, 128, 129

backyard enclosure, 157

barn cats, 178

Barn Cats, Inc., 178

behavior changes, 16, 100, 130

behavior consultant, 24, 27, 71, 76, 147, 149, 171

behavior disorders, 95

behaviorist, 24, 25, 27, 32, 37, 71, 76, 147, 149, 171, 173

Bellrock Growers, 155, 156

Bergan Star Chaser, 149

Bergan Turbo Scratcher, 149

bladder stones and crystals, 82, 84, 93, 94, 95, 99, 122

Bladder Stones and Crystals, 93

blood pressure, 83, 86, 133, 137, 138

bloody stool, 109, 112

bloody pee, 37, 75, 82

box avoidance, 124, 136, 137

box cleaning schedule, 28, 106

box cleanliness, 28, 59, 88

box location, seniors, 24, 29, 33, 84, 99, 101, 123-126, 132

box size, 29

bullying, 11, 21, 31, 55, 63, 66, 74-79, 88, 170

butt scooting, 100

C & D Pet Products, 176

cafeteria-style preference tests, 34, 35, 37, 167

calcium oxalate stones, 93

canine conflict, 80

canned food, 9, 17, 83, 93, 95, 99

Carefresh Natural Pet Bedding, 170

carpet cleaning services, 52

carpet protectors, 65

carpeting, 3, 8, 10-11, 15-16, 20, 26-28, 35, 39, 44-52, 59, 61, 65, 88, 98, 105, 129, 153, 166-171, 174-175

Cat Catcher, 148

Cat Charmer, 90, 148

Cat Dancer, 90, 148

cat fence, 157, 176

cat grass, 60, 92, 144, 155

cat litter, 8, 12, 26, 27, 33, 34, 37, 38, 95, 161, 167, 169, 170

cat repellent, 162, 163, 168

cat toys, 16, 39, 66, 74, 78, 79, 89, 91, 92, 124, 126, 143, 147, 148, 149, 150, 155, 156, 161, 176

cat tree, 71, 72, 77, 92, 129, 146, 147, 154, 160, 167

Cat Wrangling Made Easy 67, 80

cationic detergent, 48, 51

Catit Self Groomer, 66

Catit Senses 2.0 Digger, 150

catnip, 66, 67,149,150, 155,15

catnip party, 66, 155

CatSpot cat litter, 36

CatStop Ultrasonic Cat Deterrent, 64

cause stress, 87, 144

change in family, 63, 64, 71, 73, 74, 79, 87, 152, 160, 177

CheckUp, 95

chronic kidney disease, 133-135

Churchill, Winston, 55

Citrus, 8, 34, 48, 51

citrus cleaners, 48

cleaning products, dangers, 47

cleaning urine, 2, 28, 32, 34, 46-49, 51, 52, 61, 66, 106, 136, 152, 167-169

Cleanliness, 26, 28

climber, 31, 33, 39, 76, 92, 124, 128, 143, 144, 145, 157

clothes dryer, 41

clumping litter, 8, 28, 30, 35, 36, 169

clustering boxes, 39, 76

coccidia, 112

cognitive dysfunction syndrome (CDS), 99, 129-132

common sense hygiene, 59

confinement, 166, 175

conflict, 60, 63, 70, 77

conflict resolution, 76-79

conflict, clandestine, 73

conflict, direct, 60, 70

cool surfaces, 82, 170

coping options, 174

covering waste, 23, 32, 160

covered box, 25, 28, 31, 32, 76, 77, 87, 103, 169

covered box, easy escape, 31

crayon, 17

crime scene cleanup, 44

CrinkleBouncer, 148

Crunchy Feather Cat Toy, 78

Crystal Clear Litter Pearls, 95

Da Bird, 66, 78, 90, 148

declaw, 10, 37, 105, 106, 123, 178

dehydration, 112, 136

detergents, 51

deworming, 110, 112

diabetes, 102, 106-108

diarrhea, 52, 109, 136, 138

diet, 92, 93, 141

dirty clothes, 13, 38, 58, 66

dirty litter box, 27, 84, 87, 99, 103, 179

disinfectants, 49

divorce, 9

dogs, 15, 31-32, 39, 46, 56, 63, 69, 71, 73, 74, 76, 78, 80, 87,

92, 98, 103, 114-115, 126-127, 150-154, 160, 169
Drinkwell Pagoda Fountain, 134, 152
drug management, 63
drug therapy, 178
dry food, 9, 66, 83, 85, 92, 93, 148, 150
Drymate Cat Litter Mat, 39, 174
Ducky World Yeowww, 156
Egg-Cersizer Cat Toy, 150
elderly cat, 102, 106, 121, 127, 137
elevated perch, 77, 92, 154, 157, 176
encapsulators, 50
enemas, 104
environment, predictable, 89
environmental change, 130, 166
environmental enrichment, 21, 62, 79, 88, 90, 91, 132, 147, 151, 156
environmental management, 59
enzymes, 49, 50
escape route, 31, 40, 75, 80, 92
euthanasia, 105, 173, 174, 177, 178, 179
exercise, 66, 90, 124, 145, 147
Fabulon, 175
fear, 73
fear of box, 31
fear of darkness, 41
FeatherBouncer, 90
fecal float, 111-113
feces cleanup, 51
feeding schedule, 9
feline friendly flooring, 174
feline lower urinary tract

disease, 10, 81-84, 93-95, 102, 110, 121-123
feral cats, 34, 40, 51, 70, 144
Fizzion, 49
flea/heartworm preventives, 98
floor scooting, 100, 101
flooring, 52, 54, 174, 175
flooring, wood, 52, 175
flower pot, 162
food, 7, 88, 92, 109, 126, 150
food allergies, 110
food puzzles, 66, 92, 144, 150
giardia, 112, 113
Go Fur It Cat Toy, 148
Grout Boost, 175
guarding, 26, 39, 76
HandicappedPets.com, 174
heartworms, 112, 114, 115
hepatic lipidosis, 92, 108, 125
hiding places, 74, 77, 92, 144, 147, 160, 167
home base, 70, 71, 155, 156, 166
home health monitoring, 95
home range, 70
hookworms, 112
human medication, aspirin, 88, 109
human medication, ibuprofen (Advil, Midol, Motrin IB, etc.), 127, 136
human medication, Kaopectate, 109
human medication, Metamucil, 104
human medication, Naproxen (Aleve, etc.), 127
human-related problems, 72
hydration, 94, 134
hydrochloric acid, 48

hydrogen peroxide, 45, 175

hyperthyroidism, 96, 106, 109, 137-141

ideal litter box, 22

idiopathic cystitis, 37, 40, 75, 82-92, 122, 176, 179

incontinence, 100

increased thirst, 99, 137

increased urination, 99

Increasing territory, 77

inflammatory bowel syndrome, 110

interactive toys, 89, 144

kidney disease, 10, 94, 96, 99, 106, 121, 122, 133, 135, 136, 137, 138, 139, 141

Kilz Max Stain and Odor Blocker, 175

Kit4Cat Cat Urine Sample Collection Kit, 95

hierarchy, 71, 72

laxatives, 104

legal spraying station, 66

litter, pine, 8, 36

litter box avoidance, causes, 8-16, 20-32, 34-41, 43-44, 51, 59-62, 67, 71, 74-76, 79, 81-91, 94, 95, 97-103, 105, 106, 109, 111-114, 117, 121-124, 127-130, 132, 135, 137, 143-144, 152- 153, 159-162, 166-171, 176-178

litter box, changing, 38, 170, 171

litter box liners, 8, 25, 38, 39, 170

litter box locations, 39, 40

litter box, low-sided, 127

litter box odor, 27, 35

litter box, open, 7, 31, 32, 75, 161

litter box scooping, frequency, 27, 59

litter box scooping, how to, 28

litter depth, 26, 28, 170

litter mats, 8, 25, 38-39, 170

litter savings, 27

litter texture, 8, 21, 36

litter, alternative, 38, 170, 171

litter, citrus, 34, 163

litter, nonclumping, 36

litter, pellets, 105

litter, scented, 8, 25, 27, 34,, 35, 37, 39, 50, 51, 168

litter, scoopable, 28, 30, 35, 36, 96, 169

litter, silica gel, 36-37, 52, 95, 162

litter, texture, 12, 35, 37, 38, 39, 88, 132, 153, 166, 170

litter, unscented, 21, 23, 33, 36, 161, 169

Litter-Lifter litter scoop, 28

liver disease, 92, 109, 121

longhaired cats, 35, 36, 83, 119, 129

L-theanine, 90, 186

M.A.X. Endeavor Cat Scratcher, 154

making inappropriate elimination unpleasant, 20, 167

Manx, 83, 110

marking territory, 55, 100

masking odor, 48, 51

masking agents, 51

meals, 78

medicating, 88, 138, 139

medication, buprenorphine, 91, 126

medication, Fentanyl, 126
medication, acepromazine, 91
medication, buprenorphine, 91, 126
medication, Clindamycin, 114
medication, corticosteroids, 126
medication, cyproheptadine, 135
medication, fluorescein, 16, 17
medication, gabapentin, 106, 126
medication, meloxicam (Metacam), 126
medication, methimazole (Tapazole and Felimazole), 139, 141
medication, metronidazole (Flagyl), 113
medication, Mirtazapine, 135
medication, nizatidine, 104
medication, polysulfated glycosaminoglycan (Adequan), 126
medication, praziquantel and pyrantel pamoate (Drontal), 116
medication, ranitidine, 104, 135
medication, selegiline hydrochloride (Anipryl), 131, 191
medication, sulfadimethoxine (Albon), 112
megacolon, 103, 104
micro-territories, 70
mobility issues, 101, 123
molecular odor eliminators, 49
motion-activated devices, 64, 65, 162, 168

motives for spraying or peeing, 5, 8, 12, 14, 58, 59
Mugsy the swamp tour cat, 63-64
multicat home, 31, 36, 52, 67, 69, 71, 72, 75, 76, 80, 141, 157, 170, 176
multicat stress, 60
multipet home, 1, 15, 76, 90
natural eating opportunities, 92, 149
natural cleaning products, 48
nausea, 135
Neko Birbug, 78, 90, 148
Neko Pawdz, 147
Nekoflies, 78
normal feline behavior, 144
nose, sensitivity, 3, 12
Nutramax Cosequin for Cats, 127
Oasis Thirst Quencher Dog Waterer, 151
obesity, 83, 102, 103, 107, 123, 124, 125
obstruction, urinary tract, 94, 122
odor eliminators, 45-52
orthopedic injuries, 101, 123
Our Pets Batting Practice, 149
outdoor cats, 9, 29, 56, 70, 73, 144, 145, 159, 161, 162, 176
outdoor litter box, 162
outside living, 60, 157
pain, 6, 33, 35, 36, 47, 48, 67, 74, 82, 83, 88, 91, 93, 94, 99, 100, 101, 106, 112, 121, 123-170, 179
pancreatitis, 107
Pandora syndrome (see

idiopathic cystitis)
parasites, 111-116, 161
Patton, George S., 53-56, 63
pee clumps, 28, 135
peeing or marking?, 10
Peek-A-Prize Toy Box, 150
perception of safety, 40, 58, 65, 73, 76, 80, 129, 146
perimeter soiling, 58
PetSafe The Cheese, 149
phantom limb pain, 106
pheromones, 12, 44, 56, 61, 62, 66, 90, 133, 153, 156
pheromones, facial, 61, 62, 90, 169
pheromones, friendly, 56, 61, 62, 66, 80, 90, 133, 144, 156, 169
Pioneer Pet Raindrop, 134, 152
plant problems, 169
Precious Cat Long Haired Cat Litter, 36
Precious Cat Senior litter, 36, 37, 170
preference tests, 34, 35
punishment, 20, 22, 160
puppy pads, 38, 128
Purr. . .fect Fence, 157
Purrfect Arch, 66
questionnaire, 5, 6
radioactive iodine therapy, 138
real estate, 60, 71, 72, 154
redirected aggression, 73, 87
reducing stress, 22, 60, 61, 62, 88, 89
rehabilitation, 166
rehoming, 38, 176, 177
reintroduction, 78, 79
remodeling, 58, 59, 88
repel intruders, 64

respiratory issues, 47, 85, 111, 115
roundworms, 111, 112, 117
rubber bands, 17, 109
sanctuary, 78, 79, 160, 161, 162, 166, 175
sand, 161, 171
sanitary hair cut, 36
ScareCrow Motion-Activated Animal Deterrent, 64
schedules, 88, 89, 132
scratchers, 60, 66, 71, 79, 91, 92, 143, 144, 153, 154, 176
scratching, 21, 32, 60, 66, 71, 79, 87, 91, 92, 100, 143, 144, 153, 154, 160
scratching opportunities, 153
self- scooping boxes, 32
self-scooping electronic boxes, 7, 160
senior cats, 6, 29, 102, 106, 119, 121, 122, 129, 132, 137, 187
SENTRY Calming collar, 62
SENTRY Calming Spray for Cats, 90
serotonin, 90
Simple Solution Hardfloors Stain + Odor Remover, 52
situational dominance, 71
SmartCat Sky Climbers, 146
solvents, 47
spiteful misbehavior, 6, 98
spraying, 11, 12, 28, 56
squatting, 6, 8, 12-14, 19, 31, 40, 82, 128
Ssscat, 65, 168
stain removers, 46
staring, 59, 73, 77, 78
Sticky Paws Furniture Strips, 65,

154, 168
storage box, 7, 29, 128
stress, 11, 20, 22, 56, 58, 66,
    75, 77, 82, 85-92, 95, 103,
    122, 137, 155-157, 178, 192
stress, causes, 87, 144
stress, chronic, 85, 86
stress marking, changes, 59
stress medication, 91
stress reduction, 60, 88, 91
stress, effects of, 86, 89, 91,
    108, 121, 192
subcutaneous fluids, 134
subflooring, 3, 44, 45, 174
supplement,
    Activait Cat, 132
    apoaequorin (Neutricks for
        Cats), 132
    Cholodin-FEL, 132, 192
    curcumin, 132
    glucosamine, 127
    glucosamine pentosan, 91
    L-theanine, (Anxitane), 90
    Novifit, 132
    pentosan polysulfate, 91
Surefit furniture slipcovers, 174
surrendering cat, 178
tailless cats, 83, 110
tapeworms, 115, 116
target cat, 69, 73-78, 85, 178
temporary boarding, 166
territorial aggression, 62, 71, 76
territory, 11, 12, 54-57, 60, 63-
    65, 67, 70-73, 76-77, 86-87,
    92, 133, 144-145, 154-155,
    160, 167
timesharing territory, 70, 71
Tobin Farms Red Deer Antler
    Velvet, 127
toileting, 11, 156, 162, 168

toxoplasmosis, 59, 113, 114,
    117
transitioning outdoor cats
    inside, 160
treasure hunts, 149, 176
Ultimate Scratching Post, 66,
    154
ultraviolet light, 10, 13, 16
Urinalysis, 94
urinary tract
    infection, 82, 84, 110, 135
urine marking, 87
    causes, 60
    hygene, 59
    spraying, 58
urine odor, 24, 28, 33, 35, 41,
    44-45, 48-52, 56, 101, 161,
    168, 174
urine pattern
    long stream, 14
    round pattern, 10, 14
    spraying, 11, 12, 28, 56
ValleyVet.com, 135
veterinarian,
    reasons to visit, 98, 124, 129,
        138
veterinary behaviorist, 20, 34,
    44, 53, 171
video surveillance, 17
vinegar, 48
warning signs of illness, 99
water, 83, 94, 151, 169
water fountain, 83, 134, 152
water intake, 85, 151
weight loss, 100, 108, 112, 113,
    121, 124, 125
wild animals, 9, 87, 154
window perch, 77, 92, 154, 157
Wispy Close-Up Toy, 148
Zero Odor, 49, 52

ABOUT THE AUTHOR

Dusty Rainbolt, ACCBC, is past president of the Cat Writers' Association, a member of International Association of Animal Behavior Consultants and editor-in-chief for AdoptAShelter.com. She's the award-winning author of *Cat Wrangling Made Easy: Maintaining Peace and Sanity in Your Multicat Home* (a book for frustrated people dealing with the chaos of a multicat home), *Kittens For Dummies* and author of eight science fiction/fantasy novels.

Made in the USA
Columbia, SC
16 November 2018